PRAISE FOR *READING GROUP CHOICES*

"We have learned over the years that displays are a great way to encourage circulation at our small, rural library. One of our best displays is based on the wonderful literary guide published by Reading Group Choices! ... Patrons cannot wait to get their copies and start reading. We sincerely LOVE your product and feel that it helps us create one of our favorite displays EVER."
—**Gail Nartker, Sandusky District Library**

"Reading Group Choices continues to be a first-rate guide for those delicious reads that book group members enjoy reading, and that prompt the most enriching discussions." —**Donna Paz Kaufman, Paz & Associates, The Bookstore Training Group**

"I recommend Reading Group Choices as the number one starting point for book clubs. The newsletter is fantastic and I especially like the Spotlight Book Club section. It is a nice way to meet other book clubs. I am very happy with the book selections offered by Reading Group Choices. Thank you for this excellent service." —**Ana Martin, Cover to Cover Book Club, Hollywood, FL**

"Not only is Reading Group Choices a great resource for individual readers and book groups, it's also an invaluable tool for teachers looking to introduce new books into their curriculum. Reading Group Choices is a brilliant concept, well executed." —**Kathleen Rourke, Executive Director of Educational Sales and Marketing, Candlewick Press**

"I love your book, website and the newsletters! As an organizer of two book clubs, it's so great to get an early line on upcoming titles. The hardest part is waiting so long to read the book! By using recommendations from your newsletters, I can build a list of monthly book selections one whole year in advance." —**Marcia, CCSI Book Club**

"Quail Ridge Books has worked with Reading Group Choices for many years and the guide has been sought out at our twice yearly Book Club Bash. The prize bags of books have been a highlight. We are great partners in getting good books into the hands of people who love to read and discuss books."
—**René Martin, Events Coordinator, Quail Ridge Books**

D0974641

Welcome to

READING GROUP
CHOICES

In memory of Nancy Olson,
founder of Quail Ridge Books & Music
(1941-2016)

*"Shoppers would ask Nancy's advice about what to read for their book clubs.
They would come in and say, 'We want something light,' and she would say,
'No. That's not what a book club is for. You want to be challenged.
You want to feel something.'"*

—Sarah Goddin, Nancy's longtime friend and current general manager
of Quail Ridge Books, *News & Observer*, Raleigh, N.C.

Dear Readers,

Welcome to the 23rd edition of Reading Group Choices. We are excited about this selection of fiction, nonfiction, and young adult titles, and we hope these books and discussion questions inspire lively discussions all over the world! This edition includes translated works, memoirs, novels, graphic memoirs, and books that will be published in 2017 so when you plan your group's list for the year, you can plan ahead!

This year we continued to receive requests for more nonfiction and young adult recommendations so we added a nonfiction book recommendation to our monthly eNewsletter, and, like the 2016 edition, the 2017 edition provides fiction, nonfiction, and young adult sections. We are continuing to connect with debut authors and new independent publishers in order to provide you with new and unique recommendations.

Many of the books included in this edition will also be included on our website this fall and winter. Be sure to check the site and to sign up for our eNewsletter so you can hear about new titles and enter contests for signed copies and Skype chats with our authors! We also host events for reading groups at bookstores and book festivals around the country. We list upcoming dates in our eNewsletter and on our Facebook page.

Thank you to our readers for supporting and inspiring us. Thank you to our book clubs for sharing your stories. And thank you to our authors, our independent bookstores, and our friends in publishing for working so tirelessly and celebrating so effortlessly the love of the written word.

To order more copies of this edition or past editions, you can visit our store online at ReadingGroupChoices.com, or mail in the order form at the back of this book. Please visit our website, like us on Facebook, and find us on Twitter.

Here's to another year of reading, discussing, and discovering your new favorite books!

M.m

Mary Morgan
Reading Group Choices

Contents

FICTION

ALL THE STARS IN THE HEAVENS
Adriana Trigiani

The movie business is booming in 1935 when twenty-one-year-old Loretta Young meets thirty-four-year-old Clark Gable on the set of *The Call of the Wild*. Though he's already married, Gable falls for the stunning and vivacious young actress.

Far from the glittering lights of Hollywood, Sister Alda Ducci has been forced to leave her convent and begin a new journey that leads her to Loretta. Becoming Miss Young's secretary, the innocent and pious young Alda must navigate the wild terrain of Hollywood with fierce determination and a moral code that derives from her Italian roots. Over the course of decades, Alda and Loretta encounter scandal and adventure, choose love and passion, and forge an enduring bond of love and loyalty that will be put to the test when they face the greatest obstacle of their lives.

Trigiani's masterful storytelling takes us on a worldwide ride of adventure, from Hollywood to Italy, in a mesmerizing epic that is at its heart a luminous tale of the most cherished ties that bind. Brimming with larger-than-life characters both real and fictional—including stars Spencer Tracy, Myrna Loy, David Niven, Hattie McDaniel, and others—*All the Stars in the Heavens* is the unforgettable tale of one of cinema's greatest love affairs during the heyday of American moviemaking.

"A thoroughly entertaining tale that brings Hollywood's golden age alive."
—People

"Trigiani spins a tale of star-crossed lovers ... A heartwarming tale of women's lives behind the movies." —Kirkus Reviews

ABOUT THE AUTHOR: **Adriana Trigiani** is beloved by millions of readers around the world for sixteen bestsellers, including *All the Stars in the Heavens*; the blockbuster epic *The Shoemaker's Wife*; the Big Stone Gap series; *Lucia, Lucia*; the Valentine series; the Viola series for young adults and the bestselling memoir *Don't Sing at the Table*. She is the award-winning filmmaker of the documentary *Queens of the Big Time*. Trigiani wrote and directed the major motion picture *Big Stone Gap*, based on her debut novel and filmed entirely on location in her Virginia hometown, released nationwide in the fall of 2015. She lives in Greenwich Village with her family.

July 2016 | Paperback | Fiction | 480 pp | $15.99 | ISBN 9780062319203
Harper Paperbacks | HarperCollins.com | AdrianaTrigiani.com

CONVERSATION STARTERS

1. What characteristics make Loretta so successful beyond the typical "life span" of an actress in this age of Hollywood? In what ways is she the "modern woman" that Alda considers her to be?

2. How does the time and place—the Golden Age of Hollywood—affect Loretta's relationship with Clark Gable? What are the standards that are set and why? What is it in this setting that makes it so compelling? How would the circumstances change if their relationship took place in modern times? Would a story like this be as spellbinding and compelling in Hollywood today?

3. Spencer Tracy and Clark Gable play very different roles in Loretta's life, despite both being her love interests. How does each of them affect Loretta's personal growth? To what degree does her relationship with Spencer influence her later relationship with Clark? Loretta says her biggest regret is not marrying Clark Gable. Do you agree or disagree?

4. Though Alda and Loretta come from very different backgrounds, they work well together. How does Alda's upbringing and history prepare her for a life as Loretta's secretary? What values do they share? In contrast, how does Loretta's view on the nature of love differ from Alda's?

5. Despite their feelings for one another, Loretta and Clark can't make their relationship work. What stands in their way? What do you think draws Loretta to Clark? Do you think that Clark's love for Loretta was something more meaningful to him than any of the other romances/marriages he indulged in?

6. "Loretta" is a stage name; her given name is Gretchen. Only those closest to her call her by her given name, and as a public figure, she has somewhat of a double persona. How is her true self different from how she is perceived by the masses?

7. Loretta is a devout Catholic. How does her faith inform her major life decisions?

8. Why do you think Alda felt the need to tell Luca about her past, despite Loretta's advice?

9. Motherhood plays a significant role in this story. How does Loretta's relationship with Gladys influence her choices as a mother to Judy? Why do you think Alda never adopted children?

AMONG THE LIVING
Jonathan Rabb

A moving novel about a Holocaust survivor's unconventional journey back to a new normal in 1940s Savannah, Georgia

In late summer 1947, thirty-one-year-old Yitzhak Goldah, a camp survivor, arrives in Savannah to live with his only remaining relatives, the Jeslers. There, Yitzhak discovers a fractured world, where Reform and Conservative Jews live separate lives— distinctions, to him, that are meaningless given what he has been through. He further complicates things when, much to the Jeslers' dismay, he falls in love with Eva, a young widow within the Reform community. When a woman from Yitzhak's past suddenly appears—one who is even more shattered by the war than he is—Yitzhak must choose between a dark and tortured familiarity and the promise of a bright new life.

Set against the backdrop of America's postwar south, *Among the Living* grapples with questions of identity and belonging, and steps beyond the Jewish experience as it situates Yitzhak's story within the last gasp of the Jim Crow era. That he begins to find echoes of his recent past in the lives of the black family who work for the Jeslers—an affinity he does not share with the Jeslers themselves—both surprises and convinces Yitzhak that his choices are not as clear-cut as he might think.

"From its first pages, Among the Living *carries you into a particular time and setting, into the lives of people with whom you are entirely unfamiliar, and holds you there with a story that will stay with you for years to come. What a powerful, moving book."* —**David McCullough, Pulitzer Prize and National Book Award-winning author**

ABOUT THE AUTHOR: **Jonathan Rabb** is an American novelist, essayist, actor, and writer. He is the author of five novels: *The Overseer*; *The Book of Q*, and The Berlin Trilogy, a critically acclaimed series of historical thrillers set in Berlin and Barcelona between the world wars. *Rosa* won the 2006 Director's Special Prize at Spain's Semana Negra festival, and was named one of January *Magazine*'s Best Books of 2005. Rabb has taught at Columbia University, New York University, the 92nd Street Y, and is currently an instructor in the writing department at the Savannah College of Art and Design.

October 2016 | Hardcover | Fiction | 288 pp | $25.95 | ISBN 9781590518038
Other Press | OtherPress.com

CONVERSATION STARTERS

1. When Goldah arrives in Savannah he recognizes "This was the second code, the second assurance that [he] belonged" (7). What are the "codes" that signal to Goldah the mores of the town or the Jewish community the Jeslers are a part of?

2. Compare Goldah's first encounter with Mary Royal (14–19) to their interaction starting on page 44. How are the two scenes different? What causes the difference?

3. Goldah remembers his father telling him, "You wouldn't want me digging a ditch" (135). How do Goldah's father's feelings and ideas about class reflect on Jesler's and Pearl's own preoccupations with it? Are there other ways in which Goldah's life in Europe reverberate in his new life in Savannah?

4. Goldah remembers that when his father was murdered, the SS guards explained that it "was for Goldah to stand and watch. It was nothing his father had said or done. It was simply to show it could be done" (137). Do you think there is a similarity between how Goldah's father is murdered and the violence Raymond is subjected to?

5. What does Calvin mean when he says, "They tried to kill you, all a you, all at once. I seen that. But here they kill us one at a time and that's a difference" (116)? Explain the "difference" that he refers to.

6. How does the Jewish community Pearl introduces Goldah to treat him and his experience of the Holocaust? What is the difference between the Jeslers and the De la Parras? What do Goldah and Malke make of this difference?

7. How does Malke's appearance affect Goldah's life in Savannah? Why do you think Goldah is unable to identify with Malke when he so easily feels a camaraderie with Calvin and Raymond?

8. What is the difference between how Malke and Goldah react to their experiences of the Holocaust? Why do you think Goldah is able to make a home in Savannah while Malke has to leave?

9. Describe Malke. Do you think she functions as an antagonist or a villain in this novel?

10. At the end of the novel Goldah says he has two selves, "One to survive, the other to live" (297). What in Savannah has taught him how to live?

THE BURIED GIANT
Kazuo Ishiguro

From one of the most preeminent writers of our times comes *The Buried Giant*, an extraordinary new novel that poses powerful questions about love, loss, and mortality. The novel centers around an elderly couple, Beatrice and Axl, who set out on an epic journey through war-torn lands in hopes of finding their son. As they contend with the physical hardships of their journey, they also encounter danger from a variety of mystical elements: ogres, demons, and an ever-present fog that makes memory elusive. With the help of a brash yet determined knight and a mysterious young boy, they travel across lands familiar and strange, ever closer to learning their son's fate. What they end up discovering along the way, though, leads them in surprising directions that will forever alter the fabric of their relationship—as well as the history of their embattled homeland.

At once both brutal and affecting, Ishiguro's novel is a fresh take on the hero's journey. With unforgettable characters and a pace that rivets, *The Buried Giant* is sure to resonate as a classic for years to come.

"*Spectacular* ... The Buried Giant *has the clear ring of legend, as graceful, original and humane as anything Ishiguro has written.*" —**The Washington Post**

ABOUT THE AUTHOR: **Kazuo Ishiguro's** seven previous books have won him wide renown and numerous honors. His work has been translated into more than forty languages. Both *The Remains of the Day* and *Never Let Me Go* have sold more than one million copies, and both were adapted into highly acclaimed films.

January 2016 | Paperback | Fiction | 336 pp | $16.00 | ISBN 9780307455796
Vintage | PenguinRandomHouse.com

CONVERSATION STARTERS

1. In Chapter Two, Axl and Beatrice have an uncomfortable encounter with a boatman and an old woman. Discuss the significance of this interaction. How did you interpret the woman's odd behavior? How does this meeting with the boatman echo throughout the novel?

2. When Beatrice and Axl visit the Saxon village, Ivor apologizes for the fact that his community set on them like "crazed wolves" (59). At what other points in the novel is human behavior described as animalistic?

3. How does Edwin's memory of his mother change throughout the novel? Discuss the incident in which he is stuck in the barn. How does his mother's voice act as a protective force? How much of his recollection of his mother do you think is accurate versus fabricated?

4. Discuss the themes of trust and deception throughout *The Buried Giant*. How does the mist cause distrust between people? At what points do we see doubt creep into Axl and Beatrice's relationship? Their relationships with other characters?

5. Several characters are described as "warriors." What values or traits are intrinsic to this label? How does honor factor into a warrior's conduct?

6. Gawain leads Beatrice, Axl, and Edwin through an underground tunnel from the monastery that they had believed to be a place of refuge. Why do you think each character sees different things during their trek? Do you think the brutality described in this scene is imagined?

7. Beatrice and Axl have a horrifying experience while trying to ford a river. Discuss this scene, and the grotesque descriptions within it. What is the significance of Axl's interaction with the woman on the boat? Why do you think Beatrice's memory is so greatly affected during this scene? What does this part of their journey reveal about their relationship?

8. Axl and Beatrice's relationship is marked by tenderness and mutual affection throughout the novel. Were you surprised by the revelation? How did you interpret their final interactions in the last chapter of the novel?

9. Why do you think Ishiguro chose to have the final chapter of the book come from the perspective of the boatman?

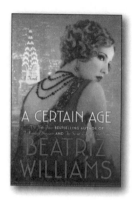

A CERTAIN AGE
Beatriz Williams

New from the bestselling author of *A Hundred Summers* **and** *Along the Infinite Sea*

As the freedom of the Jazz Age transforms New York City, the iridescent Mrs. Theresa Marshall of Fifth Avenue and Southampton, Long Island, has done the unthinkable: she's fallen in love with her young paramour, Captain Octavian Rofrano, a handsome aviator and hero of the Great War.

An intense and deeply honorable man, Octavian is devoted to the beautiful socialite of a certain age and wants to marry her. While times are changing and she does adore the Boy, divorce for a woman of Theresa's wealth and social standing is out of the question, and there is no need; she has an understanding with Sylvo, her generous and well-respected philanderer husband.

But their relationship subtly shifts when her bachelor brother, Ox, decides to tie the knot with the sweet younger daughter of a newly wealthy inventor. Engaging a longstanding family tradition, Theresa enlists the Boy to act as her brother's cavalier, presenting the family's diamond rose ring to Ox's intended, Miss Sophie Fortescue—and to check into the background of the little-known Fortescue family. When Octavian meets Sophie, he falls under the spell of the pretty ingénue, even as he uncovers a shocking family secret. As the love triangle of Theresa, Octavian, and Sophie progresses, it transforms into a saga of divided loyalties, dangerous revelations, and surprising twists that will lead to a shocking transgression ... and eventually force Theresa to make a bittersweet choice.

"Set in the Roaring Twenties in the high-society circles of New York City, Williams' story is a rousing, enjoyable read. ... Williams' historic details and detailed descriptions only add to the decadence. New money, old money and intrigue make for a lot of lively fun." —**Dallas-Forth Worth Telegram**

ABOUT THE AUTHOR: A graduate of Stanford University with an MBA from Columbia, **Beatriz Williams** spent several years in New York and London hiding her early attempts at fiction, first on company laptops as a communications strategy consultant, and then as an at-home producer of small persons, before her career as a writer took off. She lives with her husband and four children near the Connecticut shore.

January 2016 | Paperback | Fiction | 336 pp | $15.99 | ISBN 9780062404961
William Morrow | HarperCollins.com | BeatrizWilliams.com

CONVERSATION STARTERS

1. By the tone of the first few pages, did you get the sense that *A Certain Age* was set during the period between World War I and World War II? Why or why not? How does the author set the stage for the era when describing the Roaring Twenties in New York City?

2. At the beginning of the novel, Boyo is beautiful and alluring because he can't have what he most wants: Theresa. Theresa loves Boyo but knows she's not who Boyo thinks she is—she's twice his age and (at that point) married to a man with a mistress. Isn't the point of an affair to get close to a feeling you can't quite possess? Is it possible for an affair to work if both parties have nothing to lose?

3. *A Certain Age* is set in the 1920s in the era of speakeasies and bootlegging. Which scenes did you gravitate towards most: the underground parties full of flappers, smoke, and jazz of Julie Schuyler's taste, or the upper-crust soirees decorated with crinoline, lace and fancy cocktails? Do you get a sense that the author preferred writing about one over the other?

4. Many of the scenes between Boyo and Theresa, and Sophie and Octavian/Mr. Rofrano are romantic, but each for a different reason. Which scenes do you think are more convincing? What qualities make up the perfect romantic scene?

5. Sophie and Theresa are alter egos of a sort. Do you identify with one over the other? Who were you rooting for to win Octavian's heart? Did your opinion of him change throughout the course of the novel?

6. What a suspenseful ending! Did you piece any of the mystery together before the truth was revealed? What clues gave the ending away?

7. Theresa makes two choices at the end of the novel. Does it fit her character, and what does it say about the way she's evolved? Would you have made the same choice if you were in her shoes? Why or why not?

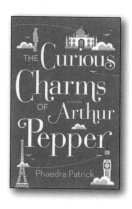

THE CURIOUS CHARMS OF ARTHUR PEPPER

Phaedra Patrick

In this poignant and curiously charming debut, a lovable widower embarks on a life-changing adventure.

Sixty-nine-year-old Arthur Pepper lives a simple life. He gets out of bed at precisely 7:30 a.m., just as he did when his wife, Miriam, was alive. He dresses in the same gray slacks and mustard sweater-vest, waters his fern, Frederica, and heads out to his garden. But on the one-year anniversary of Miriam's death, something changes. Sorting through Miriam's possessions, Arthur finds an exquisite gold charm bracelet he's never seen before. What follows is a surprising and unforgettable odyssey that takes Arthur from London to Paris and as far as India in an epic quest to find out the truth about his wife's secret life before they met—a journey that leads him to find hope, healing and self-discovery in the most unexpected places.

"Tender, insightful, and surprising ... [Arthur Pepper] will instantly capture the hearts of readers who loved The Unlikely Pilgrimage of Harold Fry, The Little Paris Bookshop, *and* The Red Notebook.*" —Library Journal* (starred review)

"Eccentric, charming, and wise, this book will illuminate your heart." —Nina George, *The New York Times* bestselling author of *The Little Paris Bookshop*

"When Arthur's grief overwhelms him ... it pierces the heart. You root for him every step of the way" —BookPage

ABOUT THE AUTHOR: **Phaedra Patrick** studied art and marketing and has worked as a stained glass artist, film festival organizer and communications manager. She is a prize-winning short story writer and now writes full time. She lives in the UK with her husband and son. *The Curious Charms of Arthur Pepper* is her debut novel.

May 2016 | Hardcover | Fiction | 354 pp | $24.99 | ISBN 9780778319337
MIRA | MiraBooks.com | Phaedra-Patrick.com

CONVERSATION STARTERS

1. What do you think the ending suggests about Arthur's mindset at the end of his journey? Is he hopeful? At peace? What do you think is next for him?

2. How does Arthur's journey change him? What does he ultimately learn about himself?

3. As Arthur discovers more about Miriam's secret life, how do you think his feelings about his marriage to her changes?

4. Why do you think Miriam never told Arthur about her life before they met? Do you think she was justified in keeping such big secrets?

EL PASO
Winston Groom

Three decades after the first publication of *Forrest Gump*, Winston Groom returns to fiction with this sweeping American epic.

Long fascinated with the Mexican Revolution and the vicious border wars of the early twentieth century, Winston Groom brings to life a much-forgotten period of history in this sprawling saga of heroism, injustice, and love. An episodic novel set in six parts, *El Paso* pits the legendary Pancho Villa, a much-feared outlaw and revolutionary, against a thrill-seeking railroad tycoon known as the Colonel, whose fading fortune is tied up in a colossal ranch in Chihuahua, Mexico. But when Villa kidnaps the Colonel's grandchildren in the midst of a cattle drive, and absconds into the Sierra Madre, the aging New England patriarch and his adopted son head to El Paso, hoping to find a group of cowboys brave enough to hunt the Generalissimo down.

Replete with gunfights, daring escapes, and an unforgettable bullfight, *El Paso*, with its textured blend of history and legend, becomes an indelible portrait of the American Southwest in the waning days of the frontier.

*"[Groom] combines military savvy with storytelling skill for a satisfying saga pitting an American railroad tycoon against Mexican revolutionary Pancho Villa ... An engaging epic that could be headed for the best-seller lists and then the big screen. This is the big one that fans have been waiting for, and they'll grab it up like they would a delicious box of chocolates." —**Booklist** (starred review)*

ABOUT THE AUTHOR: **Winston Groom** is the author of, among other books, *Forrest Gump*, *Conversations with the Enemy* (Pulitzer Prize finalist), *Shiloh 1862*, and *The Generals*. He served in Vietnam with the Fourth Infantry Division and lives in Point Clear, Alabama.

October 2016 | Hardcover | Fiction | 480 pp | $27.95 | ISBN 9781631492242
Liveright | books.wwnorton.com

CONVERSATION STARTERS

1. When we first meet Arthur Shaughnessy, he receives a telegram from his father stating, "See if you can handle it; when we first meet Pancho Villa, he is remembering the night he witnessed Halley's Comet—a sighting he interpreted as a bad omen. How did these first impressions set the tone for your reading? What did you anticipate?

2. Consider the significance of place: the juxtaposition between cities and countries, the vast landscapes, the wildlife, the extreme weather. How does the setting speak to greater themes of the novel?

3. The Shaughnessy men make a game out of racing to Mexico, the Colonel by train and Arthur by plane. Later in the novel, they find themselves in a very different race to save the children. What does this irony say about the characters?

4. Pancho Villa says, "You see, Mexico is a strange place. The things we do don't always make sense to you Americanos, but that's not the important thing. The important thing is that they make sense to us." What other moments in the novel could this quote apply to?

5. Racism plays a significant role throughout *El Paso*, with characters experiencing it to varying degrees. Colonel Shaughnessy, for example, is both a victim and an offender. How does racism inform the way different characters move through the world? Are perceptions altered?

6. Everyone wants to get their hands on Pancho Villa. Who has the highest stakes for finding him? Who did you find yourself rooting for? Against?

7. The misanthropic satirist Ambrose Bierce and the young journalist-socialist John Reed butt heads upon first meeting. What does their relationship say of the time period? What does it say of the younger and older generations in the novel?

8. How did your perception of Pancho Villa evolve throughout the book? Do you sympathize with him at any point?

9. How did knowing—or discovering in the end—that many of the characters were real people affect the way you read the story? Did the epilogue surprise you?

10. Why do you think the Colonel sacrifices himself in the end? Could this have been avoided, or was it crucial?

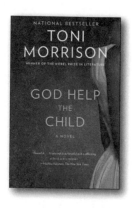

GOD HELP THE CHILD
Toni Morrison

At the center: a young woman who calls herself Bride, whose stunning blue-black skin is only one element of her beauty, her boldness and confidence, her success in life, but which caused her light-skinned mother to deny her even the simplest forms of love. There is Booker, the man Bride loves, and loses to anger. Rain, the mysterious white child with whom she crosses paths. And finally, Bride's mother herself, Sweetness, who takes a lifetime to come to understand that "what you do to children matters. And they might never forget."

A fiery and provocative novel, *God Help the Child*—the first book by Toni Morrison to be set in our current moment—weaves a tale about the way the sufferings of childhood can shape, and misshape, the life of the adult.

"Powerful... A tale that is as forceful as it is affecting, as fierce as it is resonant"
—**Michiko Kakutani,** *The New York Times*

"A tragicomic jazz opera played out in four parts. ... Morrison makes art from the cadences of human heartbreak." —The Atlantic

ABOUT THE AUTHOR: **Toni Morrison** is the author of ten previous novels, from *The Bluest Eye* (1970), to *Beloved* (1998), to *Home* (2012). She has received the National Book Critics Circle Award and the Pulitzer Prize. In 1993 she was awarded the Nobel Prize in Literature. She lives in New York.

January 2016 | Paperback | Fiction | 192 pp | $14.95 | ISBN 9780307740922
Vintage | PenguinRandomHouse.com

CONVERSATION STARTERS

1. Morrison opens *God Help the Child* with a character insisting, "It's not my fault. So you can't blame me." How does this set up what follows?

2. Multiple themes weave through the novel: childhood trauma, racism, skin color, social class, freedom. What would you say is the primary theme, and why?

3. At different points in the novel, Morrison switches from individual characters' voices to third-person narration. How does this affect the reader's understanding of what's happening?

4. Discuss Bride's friendship with Brooklyn. Over and over, Bride says how much she trusts Brooklyn, and what a good friend she is. What do these assertions tell us about Bride's character? Does it matter that Brooklyn is white and wears dreadlocks?

5. Bride testified against Sofia to please her mother. On page 42 Sweetness recalls, "After Lula Ann's performance in that court and on the stand I was so proud of her, we walked the streets hand in hand." Why did Sweetness care so much about this trial?

6. The reader's understanding of Booker is shaped by Bride's recollection of his saying, "You not the woman I want," her limited insights about him, and Brooklyn's descriptions of him as a shady character. But in Part III we learn that he's quite different from what we've imagined. What point is Morrison making here?

7. On page 180, Morrison describes Bride and Booker's thoughts about the future: "A child. New life. Immune to evil or illness, protected from kidnap, beatings, rape, racism, insult, hurt, self-loathing, abandonment. Error-free. All goodness. Minus wrath. So they believe." What do those last three words mean?

8. In an interview with Stephen Colbert, Morrison said: "There is no such thing as race ... Racism is a construct, a social construct. And it has benefits. Money can be made off of it. People who don't like themselves can feel better because of it. It can describe certain kinds of behavior that are wrong or misleading. So [racism] has a social function. But race can only be defined as a human being." In the novel, Booker says similar things. Sweetness raised Bride the way she did because of Bride's dark skin. How does this all tie together?

THE GOLDEN AGE
Joan London

Winner of the Prime Minister's Literary Award

Thirteen-year-old Frank Gold's family, Hungarian Jews, escape the perils of World War II to the safety of Australia in the 1940s. But not long after their arrival Frank is diagnosed with polio. He is sent to a sprawling children's hospital called The Golden Age, where he meets Elsa, the most beautiful girl he has ever seen, a girl who radiates pure light. Frank and Elsa fall in love, fueling one another's rehabilitation, facing the perils of polio and adolescence hand in hand, and scandalizing the prudish staff of The Golden Age.

Meanwhile, Frank and Elsa's parents must cope with their changing realities. Elsa's mother Margaret, who has given up everything to be a perfect mother, must reconcile her hopes and dreams with her daughter's sickness. Frank's parents, transplants to Australia from a war-torn Europe, are isolated newcomers in a country that they do not love and that does not seem to love them. Frank's mother Ida, a renowned pianist in Hungary, refuses to allow the western deserts of Australia to become her home. But her husband, Meyer, slowly begins to free himself from the past and integrate into a new society.

With tenderness and humor, *The Golden Age* tells a deeply moving story about illness and recovery.

"The Golden Age *is pretty much perfect.*" —*Publishers Weekly* (starred review)

"*Every character, however minor, comes to life in these pages ... London is a virtuoso.*" —*Kirkus Reviews* (starred review)

"The Golden Age *is London's most accomplished and keenly felt work to date.*" —**Geordie Williamson**, *The Australian*

ABOUT THE AUTHOR: **Joan London** is a bookseller and author living in Perth. She is the author of two short story collections, *Sister Ships*, which won *The Age* Book of the Year award, and *Letter to Constantine*, which won the Steele Rudd Award. London has written three novels, *Gilgamesh*, *The Good Parents*, and *The Golden Age*.

August 2016 | Paperback | Fiction | 224 pp | $17.00 | ISBN 9781609453329
Europa Editions | EuropaEditions.com | RandomHouse.com.au

CONVERSATION STARTERS

1. How do Frank and Elsa's parents adjust their expectations of their children, as well as their families, after Frank and Elsa are checked into The Golden Age? Does it impact their marriages?

2. Is there a parallel being drawn between the trauma of polio and the trauma of the Holocaust?

3. In your opinion, how does the Gold family's status as recent émigrés impact their descriptions and attitudes toward Perth? How is Perth compared to Budapest? How representative do you think this is of immigrants' perception of their new home?

4. How is the Australian landscape used to characterize both the Briggs and the Gold families?

5. How do the physical and psychological effects of polio translate into Elsa and Frank's adult lives?

6. How does the idea of limited mobility, not only physically from polio but also legally as minors, shape Elsa and Frank's burgeoning relationship?

7. How do the characters Margaret, Ida, and Olive represent different perspectives on motherhood, widowhood, ambition, and loss?

8. How is the Gold's struggle to assimilate into Australian life illustrated in Meyer's gravitation toward Olive?

9. What is the function of art—for the artist and for society—in this novel, especially as manifest in Sullivan, Frank, and Ida?

10. How does the Queen's visit to Perth, as well as Frank's resistance toward it, address or underscore social and political tensions during times of epidemic?

11. In your opinion, is Frank's desire to complete Seymour's poem ever achieved, or is its ambiguity the true conclusion?

GRAND HOTEL
Vicki Baum

A grand hotel in the center of 1920s Berlin serves as a microcosm of the modern world in Vicki Baum's celebrated novel, a Weimar-era best seller that retains all its verve and luster today. Among the guests of the hotel is Doctor Otternschlag, a World War I veteran whose face has been sliced in half by a shell. Day after day he emerges to read the paper in the lobby, discreetly inquiring at the desk if the letter he's been awaiting for years has arrived. Then there is Grusinskaya, a great ballerina now fighting a losing battle not so much against age as against her fear of it, who may or may not be made for Gaigern, a sleek professional thief. Herr Preysing also checks in, the director of a family firm that isn't as flourishing as it appears, who would never imagine that Kringelein, his underling, a timorous petty clerk he's bullied for years, has also come to Berlin, determined to live at last now that he's received a medical death sentence. All these characters and more, with all their secrets and aspirations, come together and come alive in the pages of Baum's delicious and disturbing masterpiece.

"Like George Grosz, Vicki Baum renders human foibles at their most pathetic, despicable, and comical, then turns her characters inside out, until we recognize our own hopes and fears refracted in them." —**Holly Brubach**

"The legacy of Baum's novel is not just the 1932 MGM film starring John Barrymore and Greta Garbo, but all those star-stuffed movies and fat popular novels ... in which some institution or event serves as the setting for the intersecting individual dramas. What distinguishes the book ... is not only its relatively modest length but the delicacy of Baum's writing ... The book is kin to both the stories of Stefan Zweig and the films of Max Ophüls, both artists who chronicled devastating loss but drew our eye to the exquisite fluidity with which the most precious things slid through their characters' elegant, manicured fingers." —*Kirkus Reviews* **(starred review)**

ABOUT THE AUTHOR: **Vicki Baum** (1888–1960) was born in Vienna. One of the world's best-selling authors, she is credited with inventing the "hotel novel" genre with *Grand Hotel*.

Introducer **Noah Isenberg** teaches at The New School. His most recent book is *Edgar G. Ulmer: A Filmmaker at the Margins*. He lives in NYC.

June 2016 | Paperback | Fiction | 304 pp | $16.95 | ISBN 9781590179673
New York Review Books | nyrb.com

CONVERSATION STARTERS

1. How would you describe the tone of the novel, and why do you think Vicki Baum chose to write the book in that style?

2. In the introduction, Noah Isenberg includes a quote from the Norwegian crime novel *Death Enters the Hotel*: "Once again it is confirmed that a large hotel is a world unto itself and that this world is like the rest of the large world. The guests here roam about in their light-hearted, careless summer existence without suspecting anything of the strange mysteries circulating among them." In what ways is Baum's hotel a "world unto itself"? Did you feel that the characters in the story viewed the hotel in that way?

3. Several of the characters in the novel are old or aging. In what ways does the theme of decay play out in the book?

4. In the introduction, Noah Isenberg writes, "The city has a distinct life of its own, like another character among the human beings who circulate within it." In what ways does Berlin function as a character in the novel?

5. On page 157, Kringelein asks the Baron, "But what is life, Herr Baron? You see, Baron, I am no longer young, and besides I am not in good health, and then you suddenly feel afraid—so afraid—of missing life altogether. I don't want to miss life, if you understand?" The Baron replies: "You can't very well miss that. It's always there. You live—and that's all there is to it." How do these differing philosophies about life develop in the book? Which characters ascribed to each man's understanding of life?

6. What was your impression of the stenographer Flämmchen? Did you find that she was a particularly modern character?

7. Describe the Baron Gaigern. How did your impression of him change when he fell in love with the ballerina Grusinskaya? What does the Baron's friendship with Kringelein reveal about him as a character?

8. What role does the veteran Dr. Otternschlag play in the novel? Did you find that his character represented something larger, socially or politically?

9. Did you find the end of the novel satisfying?

HERE COMES THE SUN
Nicole Dennis-Benn

In this radiant, highly anticipated debut, a cast of unforgettable women battle for independence while a maelstrom of change threatens their Jamaican village.

Capturing the distinct rhythms of Jamaican life and dialect, Nicole Dennis-Benn pens a tender hymn to a world hidden among pristine beaches and the wide expanse of turquoise seas. At an opulent resort in Montego Bay, Margot hustles to send her younger sister, Thandi, to school. Taught as a girl to trade her sexuality for survival, Margot is ruthlessly determined to shield Thandi from the same fate. When plans for a new hotel threaten their village, Margot sees not only an opportunity for her own financial independence but also perhaps a chance to admit a shocking secret: her forbidden love for another woman. As they face the impending destruction of their community, each woman—fighting to balance the burdens she shoulders with the freedom she craves—must confront long-hidden scars. From a much-heralded new writer, *Here Comes the Sun* offers a dramatic glimpse into a vibrant, passionate world most outsiders see simply as paradise.

*"Betrayal, forbidden trysts, innocence lost: for two Jamaican sisters wrestling with identity and womanhood, life in a seemingly postcard-perfect paradise is a lot more complicated than it looks." —**Cosmopolitan***

*"All evidence suggests that this debut deserves its ballyhoo." —**The New York Times***

"In Here Comes the Sun, *Nicole Dennis-Benn takes readers to the richly rendered shores of her Jamaican homeland ... This buzzy novel dives under the shimmering surface of paradise to expose its dark secrets." —**Elle***

ABOUT THE AUTHOR: **Nicole Dennis-Benn** has received fellowships from Hedgebrook, MacDowell, Lambda, and the Sewanee Writers Conference. Born and raised in Kingston, Jamaica, she lives with her wife in Brooklyn, New York, where she teaches writing.

July 2016 | Hardcover | Fiction | 352 pp | $26.95 | ISBN 9781631491764
Liveright | books.wwnorton.com | NicoleDennisBenn.com

CONVERSATION STARTERS

1. Nicole Dennis-Benn brings to life a Jamaica that is removed from, yet also inextricably linked with the fantasy world of the resorts. How does she create a distinct sense of place? Did the Jamaica she conjures surprise you? Did it feel foreign or familiar?

2. "God nuh like ugly," Miss Ruby warns Thandi, and her mother tells her, "nobody love a black girl." How do racism, colorism, and classism shape their society? How do these forces direct the characters' lives, thoughts, and actions?

3. How did your understanding of Margot's relationship with Delores change over the course of reading the novel? Do you find their actions toward one another understandable? Forgivable?

4. Margot, Thandi, Delores, Verdene, and Sweetness all have distinct, strong voices. Which of these women did you most sympathize (or even identify) with? Which do you hold most accountable for her actions?

5. The ever-expanding resorts threaten the homes of River Bank residents and destroy their livelihoods as farmers and fishermen. Yet the hotel business also brings jobs and, to ambitious people like Margot, the promise of prosperity. Do you consider this kind of development progress? Why or why not? Did the novel change your views?

6. How do the women in the novel relate to men? What effects do men have on women's lives and senses of self?

7. How do Jamaican religion and tradition interact with encroaching modernity on the island? Which storylines illuminate this tension?

8. What are Margot's motivations? Are they what she says they are?

9. After implementing her scheme, Margot sees Miss Novia Scott-Henry crying in the hotel bathroom, "long streaks down her face. Like scars." Why do you think Dennis-Benn uses this startling imagery?

10. Why does Margot react as she does when she finds out Thandi has been bleaching her skin?

11. What role does language play in this world, and how does Dennis-Benn use it? What social and emotional associations does the local patois carry?

12. The book's title sounds optimistic. Is that expectation borne out?

HOLD STILL
Lynn Steger Strong

Heralding the arrival of a profoundly moving new voice, *Hold Still* is a "haunting ... achingly detailed, and undeniably real" family portrait (*San Francisco Chronicle*).

When Maya Taylor, an English professor with a tendency to hide in her books, sends her daughter to Florida to look after a friend's child, she does so with the best of intentions; it's a chance for Ellie, twenty and spiraling, to rebuild her life. But in the sprawling hours of one humid afternoon, Ellie makes a mistake that she can't take back. In two separate timelines—before and after the catastrophe—Maya and Ellie must try to repair their fractured relationship and find a way to transcend not only their differences but their more troubling similarities. In tender, undulating prose, *Hold Still* explores the depths and limits of a mother's love.

*"[Strong] has a highly sensitive awareness of the special kind of disappointment—and the painfully undying connection—that comes with family." —**The New York Times***

*"Wildly evocative." —**Elle***

" ... melds psychological insight, precise plotting and limpid prose." —**Huffington Post**

ABOUT THE AUTHOR: **Lynn Steger Strong** holds an MFA in fiction from Columbia University, where she teaches Freshman Writing. She lives in Brooklyn, New York, with her husband and two young daughters.

March 2016 | Paperback | Fiction | 272 pp | $15.95 | ISBN 9781631492655
Liveright | books.wwnorton.com | LynnStegerStrong.com

CONVERSATION STARTERS

1. Although Maya has never had many friends, the few she does have are extremely important to her. Two of them are former students—one of them a nonconformist not unlike Ellie. Another is a free-spirited colleague. Given Maya's personality, did this surprise you? How do these unusual dynamics play out? Did you find them relatable?

2. Why did Ellie become so rebellious? Why does she later often secretly wish she were different? Does she make an effort to change? Why or why not?

3. Maya is simultaneously consumed by love for her children and determined to retain a separate identity. In what ways does this tension reveal itself? Do you think she succeeds?

4. *Hold Still* straddles two parts of America, two distinct worlds. How does she contrast life in New York and Florida? If you've been to either or both of these places, do her observations ring true to you?

5. What role does communication (or lack thereof) play in the novel? What thoughts do the characters leave unspoken? How does this affect their interactions and the outcome of the story?

6. Maya has always escaped into books when the real world was too overwhelming. She is also an avid runner who enjoys pushing her body to its limits. Why does she run? How do these two sides of her fit together?

7. How does Strong portray the reality, the ideal, and the meaning of parenthood? Are they the same for all of the parents in the novel?

8. Benny often sees similarities between his mother and sister. Do you see them too? How do Ellie and Maya view one another, both before the accident and after?

9. Stephen and Maya's fragile marriage begins to buckle under the weight of tragedy; Ellie uses sex as an escape; stolen glances and shared desires blur the lines of infidelity. Explore how women and men relate to one another in the novel.

10. Did you like the novel's leaps back and forth in time? Why or why not? Why do you think the author chose this structure over a traditional linear narrative?

11. Annie tells Maya that they are ultimately more responsible for the accident than Ellie is. Who do you think is most culpable and why?

IN THE UNLIKELY EVENT
Judy Blume

In this brilliant new novel—her first for adults since *Summer Sisters*—Judy Blume takes us back to the 1950s and introduces us to the town of Elizabeth, New Jersey, where she herself grew up. Here she imagines and weaves together a vivid portrait of three generations of families, friends, and strangers, whose lives are profoundly changed during one winter. At the center of an extraordinary cast of characters are fifteen-year-old Miri Ammerman and her spirited single mother, Rusty. Their warm and resonant stories are set against the backdrop of a real-life tragedy that struck the town when a series of airplanes fell from the sky, leaving the community reeling. Gripping, authentic, and unforgettable, *In the Unlikely Event* has all the hallmarks of this renowned author's deft narrative magic.

"*[A] page-turner ... Like reconnecting with a long-lost friend.*" —*The New Yorker*

"*Makes us feel the pure shock and wonder of living ... Judy Blume isn't just revered, she's revolutionary.*" —*The New York Times Book Review*

ABOUT THE AUTHOR: **Judy Blume** is one of America's most beloved authors. She grew up in Elizabeth, New Jersey, and was a teenager in 1952 when the real events in this book took place. She has written books for all ages. Her twenty-eight previous titles include *Are You There God? It's Me, Margaret*; *Forever*; and *Summer Sisters*. Her books have sold more than eighty-five million copies in thirty-two languages. She is a champion of intellectual freedom, working with the National Coalition Against Censorship in support of writers, teachers, librarians, and students. In 2004, Blume was awarded the National Book Foundation's Medal for Distinguished Contribution to American Letters. She lives in Key West and New York City.

May 2016 | Paperback | Fiction | 512 pp | $15.95 | ISBN 9781101873984
Vintage | PenguinRandomHouse.com | JudyBlume.com

CONVERSATION STARTERS

1. Discuss the environment of Elizabeth, New Jersey, before the crashes occur. How would you describe the community? How does the community band together after the first crash?

2. Throughout the book, newspaper clippings are interspersed among the text. How do those articles help to provide context for the events that occur? How did they aid your understanding of changes in Elizabeth?

3. Class and status play a role throughout the book. How does Miri see herself in the socioeconomic structure of Elizabeth? When does she feel most uncomfortable with her family's position? How does her idea of relative wealth change once she meets Mason?

4. Discuss Miri's relationship with her mother. How would you define the relationship between Miri and Rusty at the beginning of the novel? Does the relationship change once Miri has her own children?

5. *In the Unlikely Event* is arguably a novel about the crashes as much as it is one about Henry Ammerman's development as a journalist. How does Henry's career evolve over the course of the novel? Is he ever conflicted by his role in reporting the tragedy?

6. Discuss the conspiracy theories that emerge after the crashes. For the teenagers in the novel, how do these rumors act as a means of coping?

7. The crashes create a sense of palpable fear and anxiety for the residents of Elizabeth throughout *In the Unlikely Event*. How does it affect Miri on a psychological level? What about Natalie?

8. How is teen culture described throughout *In the Unlikely Event*? What influence does pop culture have on Miri and her peers? Were you able to trace any similarities between the teens of the 1950s and the teens of today?

9. Discuss the events of the reunion. Did the characters' lives turn out differently from how you would have expected?

10. Judy Blume has had a prolific career writing books for readers of all ages. How many of her previous novels, if any, have you read? How did your reading experience of *In the Unlikely Event* compare with her other works? Are you able to pinpoint anything in the writing or character development that felt distinctly "Judy Blume" in style or execution?

INTO THE SUN
Deni Ellis Béchard

Kabul—Ten Years After 9/11: After a car explodes in the city, a Japanese-American journalist discovers that its passengers were acquaintances—three fellow expats who had formed an unlikely love triangle—and becomes convinced that a deeper story lies behind the moment of violence. The investigation that follows takes the journalist from Kabul to Louisiana, Maine, Québec, and Dubai, from love to jealousy to hate—and acutely reveals how the lives of individuals overseas have become inseparable from the larger story of America's imperial misadventures.

"Béchard is the rare writer who knows the secret to telling the true story."
—**Marlon James**

*"*Into the Sun *is the sort of book I'm always hungry for—the serious novel in which the guns literally go off. Béchard makes me think of Graham Greene and Robert Stone, which is heady company, indeed."* —**Richard Ford**

"A ferociously intelligent and intensely gripping portrait of the expatriate community in Kabul—the idealists, mercenaries, aid workers and journalists circling around a war offering them promises of purpose, redemption, or cash, while the local Afghans in their orbit negotiate the ever-changing and ever-dangerous politics of the latter stages of the American war in Afghanistan. Brilliant." —**Phil Klay**

"Ambitious, elegant and filled with a kind of intelligence. Béchard explores the culture of the war zone, creating a compelling picture of that dark and turbulent place." —**Roxana Robinson**

ABOUT THE AUTHOR: **Deni Ellis Béchard** is the author of the novel *Vandal Love*, winner of the 2007 Commonwealth Writers' Prize for Best First Book; *Cures for Hunger*, a memoir about growing up with his father, who robbed banks; and *Of Bonobos and Men*, winner of the 2015 Nautilus Book Award for investigative journalism. His work has appeared in numerous magazines and newspapers, including the *LA Times*, *Salon*, *Pacific Standard*, and *Foreign Policy*, and he has reported from India, Iraq, Colombia, Rwanda, the Congo, and Afghanistan.

September 2016 | Paperback | Fiction | 456 pp | $18.00 | ISBN 9781571311146
Milkweed Editions | Milkweed.org | DeniBechard.com

CONVERSATION STARTERS

1. How did the opening description of Kabul prepare you for the story?

2. What qualities give the narrator both authority and credibility to fill in the gaps of this complicated story?

3. How does desire—controlled, indulged, denied—determine the course of the characters' experience in Afghanistan? What desire do they have in common? Who comes closest to achieving their deepest desire?

4. Consider the adversarial male/female relationships in the story. How do they reflect the greater struggle for power in the world?

5. How did the main characters' stories evolve as facts about the car bombing were revealed?

6. Which character's story changed the least? The most?

7. As the story of the bombing circles back upon itself, how does each new account reveal more about a character's motivation?

8. "How you take in the world changes how others see you" (152). How does Idris use how others see him to accomplish his goals?

9. Sexual assault plays a key role in the lives of women in the book.

10. How do the consequences of rape vary between these cultures? How are they the same?

11. Consider how sexual violence shapes women's lives in both cultures.

12. Frank encourages Shadiqa "to use everything at your disposal and not be shy about it." Does her behavior qualify as sexual harassment?

13. "War is a collision of fictions ... everyone [gets] caught in the freedom of invention" (136).

14. Is it reasonable to expect unbiased news coverage of war?

15. Is it possible to discern the truth without subjecting it to our own filters?

16. How does the book's portrayal of thrill-seeking writers affect your assessment of journalism from the front lines?

17. Did *Into the Sun* change or reinforce your view of America's involvement in Afghanistan?

JIMMY BLUEFEATHER
Kim Heacox

National Outdoor Book Award Winner

"Don't die before you're dead." –Old Keb

Keb Wisting is somewhere around ninety-five years old (he lost count) and in constant pain and thinks he wants to die. He also thinks he thinks too much. When his grandson, James, a promising basketball player, ruins his leg in a logging accident and feels he has nothing left to live for, Keb comes alive. Together with a rogue's gallery of colorful characters and a dog named Steve, they embark on a canoe journey deep into wild Alaska and into the human heart, in a story of adventure, love, and reconciliation.

"[A] splendid, unique gem of a novel." —*Library Journal* (starred review)

"Part quest, part rebirth, Heacox's debut novel spins a story of Alaska's Tlingit people and the land, an old man dying, and a young man learning to live." —*Kirkus Reviews* (starred review)

"Heacox does a superb job of transcending his characters' unique geography to create a heartwarming, all-American story." —*Booklist*

"What makes this story so appealing is the character Old Keb. He is as finely wrought and memorable as any character in contemporary literature and energizes the tale with a humor and warmth that will keep you reading well into the night." —**National Outdoor Book Award (NOBA)**

"Every page glistens with authentic genius born from Kim Heacox's wise and deep-rooted sense of place ... The characters seem like people we've known; they ring true, and feel vivid." —**Carl Safina, author of *Beyond Words: What Animals Think and Feel***

"This is not just a well-crafted picture of an elder; it is unforgettable, in the direct lineage of The Old Man and the Sea.*"* —**Doug Peacock, author of *In the Shadow of the Sabertooth***

ABOUT THE AUTHOR: **Kim Heacox** is an award-winning author and photographer. He lives in Alaska and is the author of several books written with a strong sense of place. When not playing the guitar or doing simple carpentry, he's sea kayaking with his wife, Melanie.

June 2016 | Paperback | Fiction | 564 pp | $16.99 | ISBN 9781943328710
Alaska Northwest Books | GraphicArtsBooks.com | KimHeacox.com

CONVERSATION STARTERS

1. Were you immediately hooked by Keb Wisting and drawn into the story or did you have a hard time relating to this unique character? Why?

2. Alaska roots this novel and plays a large part in the overall story line. How does the perception of Alaska as a mysterious and remote place play a part? Why can't the story have happened anywhere else?

3. Discuss the transformation of the relationship between Keb and James as the story evolves.

4. How does the struggle between tribal and environmental issues affect the story? If similar conflicts are happening where you live, what impacts have they had on you?

5. How does *Jimmy Bluefeather* shed light on Alaska Native tradition and perception of family and place? How are they caught between times and places and how are they meshing them together?

6. Is there a symbolism between James and the Canoe?

7. What do you think Steve the dog adds to the story?

8. Can you imagine yourself as a character in *Jimmy Bluefeather*? If so, which one? Or would you be a new character? What role would you play in the story?

9. There are numerous quotes in the book that Kim Heacox has dubbed "Kebisms"—which, if any, resonate for you?

10. If you were to talk with the author, what would you want to know? (Feel free to contact Kim Heacox direct @JimmyBluefeather on Facebook.)

LADY COP MAKES TROUBLE: A KOPP SISTERS NOVEL
Amy Stewart

After besting (and arresting) a ruthless silk factory owner and his gang of thugs in *Girl Waits with Gun*, Constance Kopp became one of the nation's first deputy sheriffs. She's proven that she can't be deterred, evaded, or outrun. But when the wiles of a German-speaking con man threaten her position and her hopes for this new life, and endanger the honorable Sheriff Heath, Constance may not be able to make things right.

Based on the Kopp sisters' real-life adventures, *Girl Waits with Gun* introduced the sensational lives of Constance Kopp and her unconventional sisters to an army of enthusiastic readers. This second installment, also ripped from the headlines, takes us further into the romping, riveting story of a woman who defied expectations, forged her own path, and tackled crime—and nefarious criminals!—along the way.

"A fine, historically astute novel ... The sisters' personalities flower under Stewart's pen." —The New York Times Book Review

"An unforgettable, not-to-be-messed-with heroine ... The rest is kickass history." —Marie Claire

"Stewart gives us three sisters whose bond—scratchy and well-worn but stronger for it—is unspoken but effortless." —NPR

"Fans of strong female characters will find their new favorite heroine in Constance Kopp." —Cosmopolitan

ABOUT THE AUTHOR: **Amy Stewart** is the award-winning author of seven books, including her acclaimed fiction debut *Girl Waits with Gun* and the bestsellers *The Drunken Botanist* and *Wicked Plants*. She and her husband live in Eureka, California, where they own a bookstore called Eureka Books.

September 2016 | Hardcover | Fiction | 320 pp | $26.00 | ISBN 9780544409941
Houghton Mifflin Harcourt | hmhco.com | AmyStewart.com

CONVERSATION STARTERS

1. In addition to her deputy sheriff duties, Constance serves Paterson as the jail matron. How do the expectations and requirements of this aspect of her job compare to those of her work as a deputy? How does each position speak to Constance's strengths and weaknesses.

2. In an era where women have limited options, discuss how characters like Providencia Monafo, Mrs. Heath, Aunt Adele, and Constance deal with fears and disappointments; how do they each choose to cope?

3. "Deputies follow the orders given to them by the sheriff," says Sheriff Heath (240). Those who don't, he asserts, are called "outlaws." Do you think Constance is an outlaw according to this definition? What power do titles and labels really have—can one still embody a role without "officially" owning its label?

4. Sheriff Heath goes to great pains to keep Constance's name out of the papers and keep her from public shame over losing von Matthesius. Do you think it's reckless of her to pursue the man despite the Sheriff's direct orders to the contrary? What would you have done in her place? What other "rules" does Constance break (or bend) in her life?

5. When they catch Reinhold, the messenger boy, he exclaims, "Rudy told me to watch for police, but he didn't say nothing about a lady" (234). Many characters focus on women not being able to do what a man can do, but what about the reverse? Identify the advantages, both illustrated in this novel and in general, of having a female law enforcement officer.

6. Much changes once Constance captures von Matthesius. Describe the changes between her and her family. How might things have ended if Constance had *not* caught von Matthesius? How would his escape influence how you viewed Constance's actions throughout the novel?

7. "The first line came with such tenderness that it seemed as if it was meant for each one of us," Constance thinks of the Christmas carol lyrics shared in the novel's ending. Discuss how they apply to Constance and her fellow lawmen. Why do you think the author chose to end the novel with this poignant moment?

THE MAGIC STRINGS OF FRANKIE PRESTO
Mitch Albom

Mitch Albom's most critically acclaimed novel yet is a stunningly original tale of love: Love between a man and a woman, between an artist and his mentor, and between a musician and his God-given talent.

Narrated by the voice of Music itself, the story follows Frankie Presto, an orphan born in a burning church, through his extraordinary journey around the world. Raised by a blind guitar teacher in Spain and gifted with a talent to change people's lives—using six mysterious blue strings—Frankie navigates the musical landscape of the twentieth century, from the 1950's jazz scene to the Grand Ole Opry to Elvis mania and Woodstock, all the while searching for his childhood love.

As he becomes a famous star, he loses his way, until tragedy steals his ability to play the guitar that had so defined him. Overwhelmed by his loss, Frankie disappears for decades, reemerging late in life for one spectacular yet mystifying farewell.

Part love-story, part magical mystery, *The Magic Strings of Frankie Presto* is Mitch Albom at his finest, a *Forrest Gump*-like epic about one man's journey to discover what truly matters and the power of talent to change our lives.

"A beautiful story ... Albom brings his literary magic once again."
—Huffington Post

"Carries you along like a beautiful melody." —*People*

"Hits the right notes. Albom's ... maxims about life will no doubt bring readers on a pleasantly sentimental journey about the bandmates in their lives."
—*USA Today*

ABOUT THE AUTHOR: **Mitch Albom** is a bestselling author, screenwriter, playwright, and nationally syndicated columnist. He is the author of six consecutive number one *New York Times* bestsellers—including *Tuesdays with Morrie*, the bestselling memoir of all time—and his books have collectively sold more than thirty-five million copies in forty-two languages. He has founded eight charities in Detroit and operates an orphanage in Port-au-Prince, Haiti. He lives with his wife, Janine, in Michigan.

November 2016 | Paperback | Fiction | 368 pp | $15.99 | ISBN 9780062294432
Harper Paperbacks | HarperCollins.com | MitchAlbom.com

CONVERSATION STARTERS

1. Of what significance—literal or symbolic—is it that Frankie Presto was born amidst El Terror Rojo, the Spanish civil war? How do you think the cultural restrictions and political tensions affected Frankie's childhood?

2. Throughout the novel, we get glimpses of Frankie's story from people—both real and imagined—who knew Frankie through his music. What does this array of voices and characters add to the novel? How do they add to our understanding of Frankie?

3. Cast into the river as a baby, Frankie is saved by the hairless dog. What is the role of the dog in Frankie's life?

4. Very early in his life, Frankie shows "flashes of genius" with music. How much of genius talent is given, how much is earned?

5. Consider Frankie's music teacher, El Maestro. What does he value most about music? How did losing his sight affect him? How does getting Frankie into his life fulfill him?

6. Beyond teaching Frankie how to play the guitar, how does El Maestro impact Frankie's life? What does he teach him?

7. Franco's oppressive political regime in Spain created conditions under which "art suffers." How can art be limited by politics?

8. Consider the long, romantic, and complex relationship between Frankie and Aurora York. Why do they always return to one another? What does this say about the role of forgiveness in the novel?

9. Frankie "grew up all over the place: Spain, England, Detroit, Nashville, New Orleans, Louisiana, California." How does this influence him and his music? How might different places and landscapes affect an artist?

10. Despite all his talent and success, late in his life Frankie still doesn't believe he deserves applause. Why might this be so?

11. How does Frankie and Aurora's adopted daughter, Kai, change Frankie's life? His music? What does Frankie mean when he tells Paul Stanley that "the older you get, the more you want your kids to know about you"?

12. The narrator, Music, claims that "all humans are musical." Do you agree? In what ways might this be true? What do you think defines music and what role does it play in our everyday life?

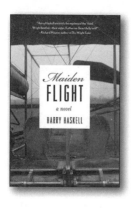

MAIDEN FLIGHT
Harry Haskell

Maiden Flight is the true-life novelization of the Wright sister who in 1926 left Orville, her world-famous and intensely possessive older brother, to marry newspaper editor Harry Haskell, the man she loved, and suffered the unhappy consequences. An international celebrity in her own right, Katharine embodied the worldly, independent, and self-fulfilled New Woman of the early twentieth century. Yet she remained in many ways a Victorian. Torn between duty and love, she agonized for months before making her devastating break with Orville at age fifty-two.

Written by the grandson of Harry Haskell, *Maiden Flight* is cast in the form of three interwoven first-person memoirs, imaginatively reconstructed from personal letters, newspaper reports, and other documents of the period—in particular, Katharine's lively and extraordinarily revealing love letters to Harry. In allowing Katharine to step outside of Wilbur and Orville's shadow, *Maiden Flight* sheds new light on the central role she played in their private lives, as well as on her often misunderstood contribution to their scientific work. Above all, the book celebrates Katharine's abundant store of what she called "human nature"—her spirited and perceptive outlook on life, her great capacity for both love and indignation, and her acute and sometimes crippling self-awareness.

"Harry Haskell unravels the mystery of the 'third' Wright brother—their sister, Katharine. Beautifully told!" —**Richard Maurer, author,** *The Wright Sister*

"Combining family lore with meticulous historical and biographical research, Haskell has crafted a lively tale of the forgotten Wright sibling. While very much of its era, the recounting of family relationships, love coming late in life, and the excitement of new technology reverberates in our own time as well." —**Tracy Barrett, author of** *Anna of Byzantium*

ABOUT THE AUTHOR: **Harry Haskell** is the grandson of Henry J. Haskell. He is the author of *Boss-Busters* and *Sin Hounds: Kansas City and Its Star*, *The Early Music Revival: A History*, and editor of *The Attentive Listener: Three Centuries of Music Criticism*.

October 2016 | Paperback | Fiction | 304 pp | $15.99 | ISBN 9781613736371
Chicago Review Press | ChicagoReviewPress.com | HarryHaskell.com

CONVERSATION STARTERS

1. When Harry unexpectedly declares his love, Katharine is forced to choose between following her heart and staying home to look after her beloved brother Orville. Think back over the difficult either-or decisions you've made in your own life. What insight do they give you into Katharine's feelings and behavior? Does your experience make you more or less sympathetic with her predicament?

2. Independent by nature and upbringing, Katharine prided herself on being unconventional in her relations with men. She supported woman suffrage, equal pay for equal work, and other aims of the women's movement, even as she assumed the time-honored role of homemaker. In what ways did Katharine subscribe to traditional Victorian values, and in what ways did she represent an emerging feminist sensibility?

3. Katharine's mother died when she was fifteen and she grew up in an all-male household. Later she served with distinction as the lone woman on Oberlin College's board of trustees. Katharine observes that she has always lived with men and doesn't regard them as "such a wonderful treat." What strategies did she adopt to survive and excel in a man's world? Do you see a connection between her interest in aeronautics and the visibility of many early women aviators?

4. The relationship between Katharine and Orville was so close that casual observers often mistook them for man and wife. Do you think Orville was justified in feeling betrayed when his sister left him to marry Harry? Would you feel differently if Katharine had been open with Orville about her wedding plans from the beginning? And do you believe that he would have taken a different view of the situation if she had given him more of a chance to get used to the idea before she married?

5. Katharine and Harry both rebelled against their strict religious upbringings and the fundamentalism of their parents. Yet religious values continued to shape their attitudes and actions. When Stef, the dashing Arctic explorer, betrays Katharine and Orville's confidence, she observes that he would be "an entirely different kind of person if he had grown up in the wholesome surroundings Harry had as a young man." What is the foundation of Katharine's moral code, and how does it manifest itself in her relationships with Orville, Harry, and Stef?

THE MIRACLE ON MONHEGAN ISLAND

Elizabeth Kelly

The best-selling, award-winning author of *The Last Summer of the Camperdowns* returns with another rollicking, summertime family saga.

When Spark—the rakish prodigal son—returns unannounced to the dilapidated family home on Maine's Monhegan Island, his arrival launches one unforgettable summer. During his absence, his gentle brother and shrewd, fork-tongued father Pastor Ragnar have been caring for Spark's son, Hally. A temperamental adolescent emboldened by tales of his father's mischief, Hally is careening through an identity crisis when he stuns his family by claiming to have had a spiritual vision. Though Spark is permanently dubious, Pastor Ragnar pounces on the chance to revitalize his flagging church. Hally is shoved into the spotlight and, in the frenzy that follows, this fragile family of fathers and sons is pushed to the brink.

Narrated in larger-than-life, crackling prose by the charismatic family dog, *The Miracle on Monhegan Island* is another uproarious and outrageous must-read summer blockbuster from Elizabeth Kelly.

"[A] tragicomic romp set off the coast of Maine. The best part? Its canine narrator is a snobbish shih tzu named Ned." —**O, The Oprah Magazine**

"Ned is an excellent guide to the Monahan world ... Man's best friend turns out—no spoiler alert needed—to be a most reliable narrator." —**The New York Times Book Review**

"Serious and thought-provoking, shot through with dark humor and dark observations on religion and faith ... The Miracle on Monhegan Island builds slowly from a story about a dysfunctional family to a novel about obsession, religious fervor and mental illness — and the sometimes very fine line between them. Even with a canine storyteller, this is one of the meatier books of the summer." —**Minneapolis Star Tribune**

ABOUT THE AUTHOR: **Elizabeth Kelly** is the best-selling author of *The Last Summer of the Camperdowns* (finalist for the New England Society Book Award) and *Apologize, Apologize!*. She lives in Merrickville, Ontario, with her husband, five dogs, and three cats.

May 2016 | Hardcover | Fiction | 336 pp | $25.95 | ISBN 9781631491795
Liveright | books.wwnorton.com

CONVERSATION STARTERS

1. Why do you think Elizabeth Kelly chose to narrate the story from a dog's perspective? What does this accomplish? Do you feel that Ned is a reliable narrator?

2. Ned is very observant, even judgmental, about his fellow dog breeds. Does this serve merely as comic relief, or something more? How does his own breed affect his personality, and how might this relate to the longstanding familial ties on Monhegan Island?

3. Ned says of Pastor Ragnor, "You can't beat the combination of a man with wicked margins who plays at being good." Do you believe that Pastor Ragnor is "wicked" at heart? Why or why not?

4. Do you think Hally is lying about the apparition, among other things? Why might he feel the need to lie?

5. Describe the island the Monahan family has lived on for generations. How do you think it relates to the story?

6. Why do you think Spark left for so long and has chosen this moment to return? Was his absence properly explained?

7. There are a lot of absent female characters in this story: Hally has lost his mother—the woman Spark loved so dearly—and his grandmother. Hugh doesn't have a partner of his own, nor has Pastor Ragnor found a replacement for Hally's grandmother. How does this loss affect the men of the Monahan family?

8. The idea of certain belief—of proof, loyalty, and truth—is questioned throughout the novel. List several instances and describe. Which character's beliefs do you find most relatable?

9. Spark is mocked by his father for being an "idealist." Which character do you think best fits that description and why?

10. As a young boy coming into his own, Hally is concerned about pleasing those around him, while seemingly eager to test his own boundaries. What are Hally's biggest worries, and why?

11. Do you agree with Ned's suspicion that Spark had always secretly believed Hally, while Pastor Ragnor never had?

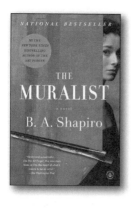

THE MURALIST
B. A. Shapiro

From the author of *The New York Times* bestseller *The Art Forger* comes a thrilling new novel of art, politics, history, and love.

When Alizée Benoit, a young American painter working for the Works Progress Administration (WPA), vanishes in New York City in 1940, no one knows what happened to her. Not her Jewish family living in German-occupied France. Not her arts patron and political compatriot, Eleanor Roosevelt. Not her close-knit group of friends and fellow WPA painters, including Mark Rothko, Jackson Pollock, and Lee Krasner. And, some seventy years later, not her great-niece, Danielle Abrams, who while working at Christie's auction house uncovers enigmatic paintings hidden behind works by those now famous Abstract Expressionist artists. Do they hold answers to the questions surrounding her missing aunt?

"Vibrant and suspenseful." —The Washington Post

"Shapiro captivated us in 2012 with her 'addictive' novel The Art Forger. *Now, she's back with another thrilling tale from the art world, set right on the brink of World War II." —Entertainment Weekly*

"The Muralist elevates Shapiro to an even higher plane and is sure to be a crowning touch in an already celebrated career." —BookPage

"The Muralist is, like What She Left Behind *by Ellen Marie Wiseman or* Orphan Train *by Christina Baker Kline, a historical novel that brings the 20th century to life." —USA Today*

"Mystery and historical fiction lovers ... will find this a riveting read." —Library Journal (starred review)

"Shapiro follows the enthusiastically received The Art Forger *with an even more polished and resonant tale. [Her] novel of epic moral failings is riveting, gracefully romantic, and sharply revelatory; it is also tragic in its timeliness as the world faces new refugee crises." —Booklist* (starred review)

ABOUT THE AUTHOR: **B. A. Shapiro** has taught sociology at Tufts University and creative writing at Northeastern University. She lives in Boston with her husband, Dan, and their dog, Sagan.

October 2016 | Paperback | Fiction | 368 pp | $15.95 | ISBN 9781616206437
Algonquin Books | Algonquin.com | BAShapiroBooks.com

CONVERSATION STARTERS

1. *The Muralist* exposes many facts about the situation in the United States before World War II, including the denial of visas to qualified refugees, the majority of the country's opposition to entering the war, and the open discrimination against Jews. Did you find any of this surprising? How has history generally portrayed this prewar period in America?

2. The issue of refugees running from war and oppression is as current today as it was during World War II. What similarities and differences to do you see between nations' responses today and those before World War II? What about in attitudes among U.S. citizens?

3. The author places Alizée, a fictional character, among the real-life artists who created the Abstract Expressionist movement in New York in the 1940s. How did living there at that time inform their art? Is there something quintessentially American about Abstract Expressionism?

4. Alizée and her friends are employed by the Federal Art Project, a New Deal program funded by the government to give work to artists. Do you think a government program like this could happen in today's political climate? How are art and artists valued or supported differently in today's society?

5. Alizée wants to believe that art can change the world. Does art have the power to affect history? Are there examples of its doing so in the past?

6. Alizée decides to be part of an assassination attempt in the hopes of thwarting a greater wrong. Do you agree with what she does? Are there times when such decisions are justifiable? What was her state of mind when she made the decision?

7. How might Alizée's life have been different if she had lived in the twenty-first century? Would her artistic dreams have been realized? How does Alizée's artistic life compare with that of her grandniece Danielle?

8. When Danielle finds out the truth about what happened to her aunt, she seems able to become the artist she was meant to be. Why? Which was more important: finding the answer, or asking the question in the first place?

9. Were you surprised at how Alizée's life turned out? Relieved? How do you think Alizée felt about it? How did her art define her life, even amid drastic change?

THE NIGHT SISTER
Jennifer McMahon

For three girls in the tiny town of London, Vermont, the summer of 1989 will change their lives forever. Piper and her little sister, Margot, are best friends with Amy, whose family owns the once-spectacular Tower Motel. Now a dilapidated relic, it's still a paradise for the girls, packed with mysterious treasures from the motel's heyday that make their imaginations run wild. But one day they make a horrific discovery about Amy's aunt, who disappeared in the 1960s just after her eighteenth birthday. Everyone said she had run off to Hollywood to live out her dream of becoming Alfred Hitchcock's next star, but when the girls find evidence of foul play, the revelation shatters their friendship.

Twenty-five years later, the secret comes back to haunt them when Amy's house turns into a violent crime scene. Is Amy at the root of this evil, or is her reclusive mother, Rose, to blame? And what happened between Rose and her sister all those years ago, setting in motion a legacy of bloodshed? Packed with the gripping plot twists and stirring atmosphere that have made Jennifer McMahon a bestselling master of suspense, *The Night Sister* will captivate you on every page.

"Chilling ... A powerful story of childhood friendship and sisterhood ... Dark and compelling." —BookPage

ABOUT THE AUTHOR: **Jennifer McMahon** is the author of seven novels, including *The New York Times* best-sellers *Promise Not to Tell* and *The Winter People*. She graduated from Goddard College and studied poetry in the MFA Writing Program at Vermont College.

March 2016 | Paperback | Fiction | 512 pp | $15.95 | ISBN 9780804169974
Anchor | PenguinRandomHouse.com | Jennifer-McMahon.com

CONVERSATION STARTERS

1. Sylvie and Rose are rivals, while Piper and Margot have a close bond. What determines whether sisters get along? How do the siblings in the book compare to yours?

2. Amy, Piper, and Margot are first-rate sleuths at age twelve. What's special about that age? Are adolescents better than their parents at seeing the truth and having an open mind?

3. Discuss the novel's interwoven timelines. Would you rather grow up in the 21st century, the 1950s, or the 1980s? In *The Night Sister*, what stays the same throughout all three eras?

4. What fuels Jason's attraction to Amy? How do his feelings about her change throughout their lifetimes?

5. How was your reading affected by Sylvie's letters to Alfred Hitchcock, and the real-life connection to Vermont in *The Trouble with Harry*? How do you think Hitchcock and his staff would have responded to her letters?

6. What were your theories about Fenton? How did your opinion of him shift?

7. With echoes of *Psycho*'s Bates Motel, what makes the Tower Motel a powerful setting for this storyline? What did the tower represent to each generation? What did you expect the 29th room to look like?

8. Compare the novel's three marriages: Charlotte and Clarence, Amy and Mark, Margot and Jason. What are the greatest strengths and vulnerabilities in these relationships?

9. What did you believe about the moth Rose keeps in a jar?

10. "Mare" is an Old English word, not an invention of the author; we use it when we talk about nightmares. How did you react to Oma's lessons about mares? What do you believe about the tangible nature of evil?

11. What do you predict for Rose and Lou? As mothers, did Charlotte and Amy do the right thing?

12. At the heart of the novel is a legacy of secrecy. Are there any long-held secrets in your family? What would it take to be ostracized by your relatives?

13. How does *The Night Sister* enhance your experience of Jennifer McMahon's previous novels? What is unique about the way her characters confront the unknown?

THE OTHER EINSTEIN
Marie Benedict

In the tradition of *The Paris Wife* and *Mrs. Poe*, *The Other Einstein* offers us a window into a brilliant, fascinating woman whose light was lost in Einstein's enormous shadow. It is the story of Einstein's wife, a brilliant physicist in her own right, whose contribution to the special theory of relativity is hotly debated and may have been inspired by her own profound and very personal insight.

Mileva Maric has always been a little different from other girls. Most twenty-year-olds are wives by now, not studying physics at an elite Zurich university with only male students trying to outdo her clever calculations. But Mileva is smart enough to know that, for her, math is an easier path than marriage. And then fellow student Albert Einstein takes an interest in her, and the world turns sideways. Theirs becomes a partnership of the mind and of the heart, but there might not be room for more than one genius in a marriage.

"Could the theory of relativity actually have been conceived by "the other Einstein"? In this fascinating and thoughtful novel, we learn that this is more than possible." —B.A. Shapiro, *The New York Times* bestselling author of *The Art Forger* and *The Muralist*

"Phenomenal and heartbreaking, and phenomenally heartbreaking." —Erika Robuck, National Bestselling Author of *Hemingway's Girl*

ABOUT THE AUTHOR: **Marie Benedict** is a lawyer with more than ten years' experience as a litigator at two of the country's premier law firms and for Fortune 500 companies. She is a magna cum laude graduate of Boston College with a focus in history and art history and a cum laude graduate of the Boston University School of Law. She lives in Pittsburgh with her family.

October 2016 | Hardcover | Fiction | 304 pp | $25.99 | ISBN 9781492637257
Sourcebooks Landmark | Sourcebooks.com | AuthorMarieBenedict.com

CONVERSATION STARTERS

1. Discuss the various ways that gender affects the characters in this novel. Do you think gender would influence Mileva's life in the same way if she lived today?

2. This novel can be seen as a quest for understanding, a search for the divine in the natural order of the world. How does the study of math and physics become this quest for Albert and Mileva? Are they, either separately or together, successful in their crusade? Does unpuzzling life's mysteries have disparate meanings to them?

3. Betrayal is a recurrent motif in the book and an unfortunate reality in Mileva's life. What forms of betrayal does she experience? How does her reaction to those betrayals propel the story forward, for better or worse? Has Mileva engaged in betrayal herself?

4. Discuss the setting of the book, a world on the brink of astounding scientific discoveries, political upheaval, and ultimately horrible World War I atrocities. Does this historical setting affect the characters? What role, if any, does it play in shaping their lives?

5. From a very young age, Mileva assumes that she will never marry due to her physical disability. How is this disability both a blessing and a curse? How does her limp impact her differently at different life stages?

6. Mileva and Albert are drawn to each other from the beginning of their years together at Polytechnic. What qualities compel them toward one another? Is their relationship "inevitable," as Mileva believes?

7. The loss of Lieserl impacts Mileva tremendously, yet she doesn't fully share her feelings with Albert. Why does she keep her devastation from him? Do you think she should have been more open with him?

8. On several occasions throughout the novel, the characters undergo metamorphoses. What are Mileva's changes, and what instigates them? Do some of them frustrate you or take too long? Does Albert change during the course of the novel? If so, how would you describe his evolution?

9. Albert Einstein is arguably one of the most famous figures of the twentieth century, but *The Other Einstein* shares a story about him that you might not have otherwise heard. Did this novel change your perception of him, or about the stories we are told regarding other women in history?

OUR SOULS AT NIGHT
Kent Haruf

In the familiar setting of Holt, Colorado, home to all of Kent Haruf's inimitable fiction, Addie Moore pays an unexpected visit to a neighbor, Louis Waters. Her husband died years ago, as did his wife, and in such a small town they naturally have known of each other for decades; in fact, Addie was quite fond of Louis's wife. His daughter lives hours away, her son even farther, and Addie and Louis have long been living alone in empty houses, the nights so terribly lonely, especially with no one to talk with. But maybe that could change? As Addie and Louis come to know each other better—their pleasures and their difficulties—a beautiful story of second chances unfolds, making *Our Souls at Night* the perfect final installment to this beloved writer's enduring contribution to American literature.

"Lateness—and second chances—have always been a theme for Haruf. But here, in a book about love and the aftermath of grief, in his final hours, he has produced his most intense expression of that yet ... Packed into less than 200 pages are all the issues late life provokes." —**John Freeman**, *The Boston Globe*

ABOUT THE AUTHOR: **Kent Haruf** is the author of five previous novels (and, with the photographer Peter Brown, *West of Last Chance*). His honors include a Whiting Foundation Writers' Award, the Mountains & Plains Booksellers Award, the Wallace Stegner Award, and a special citation from the PEN/Hemingway Foundation; he was also a finalist for the National Book Award, the *Los Angeles Times* Book Prize, and *The New Yorker* Book Award. He died in November 2014, at the age of seventy-one.

June 2016 | Paperback | Fiction | 192 pp | $15.00 | ISBN 9781101911921
Vintage | PenguinRandomHouse.com

CONVERSATION STARTERS

1. What does the title mean?

2. The novel begins with the word "and": "And then there was the day when Addie Moore made a call on Louis Waters." What do you imagine came before it?

3. Kent Haruf was known for using simple, spare language to create stories of great depth. How does the modest action in *Our Souls at Night* open onto larger insights about getting older?

4. On page 52, Louis describes his relationship with Addie to his daughter, "It's some kind of decision to be free. Even at our ages." Why does he feel freer with Addie than he does alone? How does his behavior become more uninhibited as the novel progresses?

5. When Louis confesses that he wanted to be a poet, what effect does it have on Addie's opinion of him? And on your opinion?

6. On page 145, Addie mentions the Denver Center for the Performing Arts production of *Benediction*, based on the author's own novel. Addie and Louis discuss the fact that it's set in Holt, the fictional town in which they live. Why do you think Haruf slipped this into the story?

7. At the end of that conversation, Addie says, "Who would have thought at this time in our lives that we'd still have something like this. That it turns out we're not finished with changes and excitements. And not all dried up in body and spirit" (147). What point is Haruf making?

8. In his final interview, conducted a few days before his death, Haruf discussed *Our Souls at Night*: "The idea for the book has been floating around in my mind for quite a while. Now that I know I have, you know—a limited time—it was important to me to try to make good use of that time. So I went out there every day. Typically, I have always had a story pretty well plotted out before I start writing. This time I knew generally where the story was going, but I didn't know very many of the details. So as it happened, I went out every day trusting myself to be able to add to the story each day. So I essentially wrote a new short chapter of the book every day. I've never had that experience before. I don't want to get too fancy about it, but it was like something else was working to help me get this done. Call it a muse or spiritual guidance, I don't know. All I know is that the trust I had in being able to write every day was helpful." How does reading this affect your understanding of the book?

THE PARIS ARCHITECT
Charles Belfoure

A *New York Times* bestseller

A thrilling debut novel of World War II Paris, from an author who's been called "an up and coming Ken Follett" by *Booklist*.

In 1942 Paris, gifted architect Lucien Bernard accepts a commission that will bring him a great deal of money—and maybe get him killed. But if he's clever enough, he'll avoid any trouble. All he has to do is design a secret hiding place for a wealthy Jewish man, a space so invisible that even the most determined German officer won't find it. He sorely needs the money, and outwitting the Nazis who have occupied his beloved city is a challenge he can't resist.

But when one of his hiding spaces fails horribly, and the problem of where to hide a Jew becomes terribly personal, Lucien can no longer ignore what's at stake. *The Paris Architect* asks us to consider what we owe each other, and just how far we'll go to make things right.

"A beautiful and elegant account of an ordinary man's unexpected and reluctant descent into heroism during the second world war." —**Malcolm Gladwell**

"The Paris Architect infiltrated my imagination for weeks. I dreamed about this novel." —**Jenna Blum**, *The New York Times* bestselling author of *Those Who Save Us*

"The characters are well drawn, and at the end of the story, the reader will be satisfied that some people—even the worst—may not be what they seem." —*New York Journal of Books*

ABOUT THE AUTHOR: An architect by profession, **Charles Belfoure** has published several architectural histories, one of which won a Graham Foundation Grant for architectural research. He graduated from the Pratt Institute and Columbia University, and he taught at Pratt as well as at Goucher College in Baltimore, Maryland. His area of specialty is historic preservation. He has been a freelance writer for *The Baltimore Sun* and *The New York Times*. He lives in Maryland.

July 2014 | Paperback | Fiction | 400 pp | $14.99 | ISBN 9781402294150
Sourcebooks Landmark | Sourcebooks.com | CharlesBelfoure.com

CONVERSATION STARTERS

1. Why did the majority of people in France refuse to help the Jews during World War II?

2. In the beginning of the novel, Lucien didn't care about what happened to the Jews. Discuss how his character evolved throughout the novel. How did your opinion of him change?

3. Many spouses abandoned each other because one was Jewish. What did you think when Juliette Trenet's husband left her? Is there any defense for what he did?

4. Most fiction and films portray Nazis as monsters during World War II. Do you believe that some German military men secretly hated or doubted what they were doing? Does following the crowd make these men just as bad as those who carried out their duties without conscience?

5. Discuss the unusual relationship between Lucien and Herzog. Can two men from warring countries be friends?

6. Lucien was already taking an enormous risk by hiding Jews for Manet; why do you think he agreed to take in Pierre?

7. What was your impression of Father Jacques? What kind of role do you think faith plays throughout the novel?

8. Adele had no qualms about sleeping with the enemy. Why would she take such a risk?

9. Bette could have her pick of men but chose Lucien. Discuss what made him special in her eyes. What are the most important qualities you look for in a friend/significant other? Would you be willing to compromise on any of these qualities? For what?

10. If you were a gentile living under the Nazis in World War II, do you think you would have had the courage to hide Jews? What consequences are you willing to face to help others?

11. If you were under the stairs in the Geibers' place during the Gestapo's search, how would you have reacted?

12. Schlegal was disappointed that the people he tortured always talked. What do you think were the motivations behind someone who talked and someone who didn't? If you were in a situation where someone was trying to get information from you, what would be the final straw to make you talk?

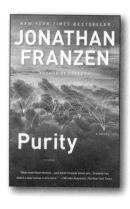

PURITY
Jonathan Franzen

A magnum opus for our morally complex times from the author of *Freedom*

In *Purity*—an epic novel of youthful idealism and disturbing realities—the acclaimed author of *The Corrections* and *Freedom* vividly imagines a world of journalists and leakers, Germans and Californians, mega-wealthy titans and homeowners in foreclosure. As she tries to navigate adulthood, Purity "Pip" Tyler embarks on a quest to discover her father's identity—and to pay down her $130,000 student-loan debt. Squatting with anarchists in a house in Oakland, she is led to the Sunlight Project, an organization whose goal is to expose the secrets of high-profile hypocrites from around the globe. The project is the brainchild of a charismatic, possibly unhinged provocateur who came of age in East Germany before the fall of the Berlin Wall. As Pip immerses herself more deeply in his group, she tests the limits of her resilience, bringing to light unexpected truths about the quest for truth itself.

A masterwork by one of the major writers of our time, *Purity* follows its characters through landscapes as contemporary as the omnipresent Internet and as ancient as the war between the sexes. A daring and penetrating book sure to spark discussion among any group.

"Franzen's prose is alive with intelligence ... the ride is exhilarating." —**Caleb Crain, *The Atlantic***

"Mr. Franzen's most fleet-footed, least self-conscious and most intimate novel yet ... Mr. Franzen has added a new octave to his voice." —**Michiko Kakutani, *The New York Times***

"In Purity *Franzen writes with a perfectly balanced fluency ... offer[ing] a constantly provocative series of insights."* —**Ron Charles, *The Washington Post***

ABOUT THE AUTHOR: **Jonathan Franzen** is the author of *Purity* and four other novels, most recently *The Corrections* and *Freedom*, and five works of nonfiction and translation, including *Farther Away* and *The Kraus Project*. He is a member of the American Academy of Arts and Letters, the German Akademie der Künste, and the French Ordre des Arts et des Lettres.

August 2016 | Paperback | Fiction | 608 pp | $17.00 | ISBN 9781250097101
Picador | us.macmillan.com/picador | us.macmillan.com/author/jonathanfranzen#

CONVERSATION STARTERS

1. From the Sunlight Project to Purity Tyler herself, how is purity defined throughout the novel? Are any of these definitions realistic, or are they steeped in youthful idealism? What is at the root of the characters' impurities?

2. How does the notion of simultaneously benevolent and sinister intentions play out in *Purity*? Who are the book's most powerful characters? How is their power derived: Secrets? Money? Integrity?

3. How would you have answered Annagret's questionnaire? What do Purity's responses say about her?

4. What does *Purity* say about humanity's capacity to exploit, and to redeem?

5. How are sex and trust interwoven in *Purity*? In the novel, is there a difference between the way men and women pursue their desires?

6. Discuss *Purity*'s images of mothering, especially between Katya and Andreas, Clelia and Tom, and Penelope and Purity. What accounts for the volatility in these relationships?

7. In their quest to expose the truth, are Tom and Andreas equally admirable? Is Leila's investigative journalism on nuclear warheads more useful than the Sunlight Project's leaked emails? Are the real-world hackers Julian Assange and Edward Snowden heroes?

8. Was Andreas right to bludgeon Horst on Annagret's behalf? How do his motivations compare to those of Tom's father when he rescued Clelia?

9. How did your opinion of Anabel shift as you read about her from different points of view? Is she insane or noble—or both?

10. Like Purity, the Pip who inhabits Charles Dickens's *Great Expectations* faces quandaries of hidden identities and tainted money. How do the dilemmas of the Information Age compare to those of the past?

11. Under what circumstances would you turn down a billion-dollar trust fund? What do we learn about the characters through their perceptions of money and justice?

12. What does the closing scene tell us about irreconcilable differences? What enables Purity to do better than her parents?

THE READERS OF BROKEN WHEEL RECOMMEND
Katarina Bivald

A *New York Times* Bestseller, Amazon Best Book of the Month, The International Bestseller, An Indie Regional Bestseller, A National Indie Bestseller, #1 Indie Next Pick, #2 LibraryReads Pick

Once you let a book into your life, the most unexpected things can happen ...

Broken Wheel, Iowa, has never seen anyone like Sara, who traveled all the way from Sweden just to meet her book-loving pen pal, Amy. When she arrives, however, she finds Amy's funeral guests just leaving. The residents of Broken Wheel are happy to look after their bewildered visitor—there's not much else to do in a dying small town that's almost beyond repair.

You certainly wouldn't open a bookstore. And definitely not with the tourist in charge. You'd need a vacant storefront (Main Street is full of them), books (Amy's house is full of them), and ... customers.

The bookstore might be a little quirky. Then again, so is Sara. But Broken Wheel's own story might be more eccentric and surprising than she thought.

A heartwarming reminder of why we are booklovers, this is a sweet, smart story about how books find us, change us, and connect us.

*"Heartwarming ... " —**People***

"A manifesto for booksellers, booklovers, and friendship ... one of these books you want to live in for a while." —**Nina George**, *The New York Times* **bestselling author of** *The Little Paris Bookshop*

"Charmingly original ... sweet, quirky." —**Bethanne Patrick**, *The Washington Post*

*"Warm-hearted" —**Woman's Day***

ABOUT THE AUTHOR: **Katarina Bivald** lives outside of Stockholm, Sweden. This is her first novel. She grew up working part-time in a bookshop.

January 2016 | Paperback | Fiction | 400 pp | $16.99 | ISBN 9781492623441
Sourcebooks Landmark | Sourcebooks.com | KatarinaBivald.se/en/

CONVERSATION STARTERS

1. Sara and Amy develop a close relationship through exchanging letters. Have you ever had a pen pal? How might a friendship conducted entirely through writing be different than an in-person relationship?

2. Even though we never met Amy in person, we get to know her through her letters to Sara. How did her letters influence your understanding of Amy and Sara's relationship?

3. How might Sara's visit have been different if Amy had been alive when she arrived?

4. Why do you think everyone in Broken Wheel felt so responsible for looking after Sara when she arrived?

5. Broken Wheel is a dying town, and a bookstore brings it back to life. How accurately do you think *The Readers of Broken Wheel Recommend* portrays small town America? Have you ever been to or lived in a place like Broken Wheel?

6. There is a strong rivalry between Broken Wheel and Hope. How do you think the residents of Hope viewed the people of Broken Wheel? How were their perceptions changed once the bookstore opened?

7. Sara arranges the books in her shop through unconventional genre names, including "Sex, Violence and Weapons" and "For Friday Nights and Lazy Sundays." What are some creative categories you might use to group your favorite books together?

8. Why do you think Sara was so reluctant to return to Sweden? What was missing from her life that she found in Broken Wheel?

9. Why do you think Caroline and Josh felt so much pressure to keep their relationship a secret?

10. *The Readers of Broken Wheel Recommend* focuses on how books can change lives. How have books affected your life? Is there one book in particular that changed the way you see the world?

11. If you were to open a bookstore, what are some of the books you would absolutely have to have for sale?

12. Where do you think Sara, Tom, and the rest of the residents of Broken Wheel will be in five years? What do you think will have changed, and what will stay the same?

THE SECRET CHORD
Geraldine Brooks

A rich and utterly absorbing novel about the life of King David, from the Pulitzer Prize-winning author of *People of the Book* and *March*. With more than two million copies of her novels sold, *The New York Times* bestselling author Geraldine Brooks has achieved both popular and critical acclaim. Now, Brooks takes on one of literature's richest and most enigmatic figures: a man who shimmers between history and legend. Peeling away the myth to bring David to life in Second Iron Age Israel, Brooks traces the arc of his journey from obscurity to fame, from shepherd to soldier, from hero to traitor, from beloved king to murderous despot and into his remorseful and diminished dotage.

"The Secret Chord—*a thundering, gritty, emotionally devastating reconsideration of the story of King David—makes a masterly case for the generative power of retelling ... some of the magic here has to do with setting and time—for sensory dramatics, it's hard to compete with the Iron Age Middle East ... but Brooks's real accomplishment is that she also enables readers to feel the spirit of the place." —The New York Times*

"*A page turner ... Brooks is a master at bringing the past alive ... in [her] skillful hands the issues of the past echo our own deepest concerns: love and loss, drama and tragedy, chaos and brutality.*" —**Alice Hoffman**, *The Washington Post*

ABOUT THE AUTHOR: **Geraldine Brooks** was born and raised in Australia. After earning her master's degree from Columbia School of Journalism, Brooks covered crises in the Middle East, Africa, and the Balkans for *The Wall Street Journal*. She published her first novel, *Year of Wonders*, in 2001, and won the Pulitzer Prize in fiction in 2006 for her second novel *March*. Brooks is also the author of the novels *People of the Book* (2008) and *Caleb's Crossing* (2011) and has wrote the acclaimed nonfiction works *Nine Parts of Desire* and *Foreign Correspondence*. She lives with her husband and two sons in Martha's Vineyard.

October 2016 | Paperback | Fiction | 352 pp | $16.00 | ISBN 9780143109761
Penguin Books | PenguinRandomHouse.com | GeraldineBrooks.com

CONVERSATION STARTERS

1. Natan's first prophecy spares him from certain death but also sets him apart from other men. Is his ability a gift or a curse?

2. How does David's childhood inform your understanding of the man he will become?

3. What might it mean that God chose to bestow so much upon a man as imperfect as David?

4. Do you believe that some people are chosen to speak in God's name? What role do prophets play in the events of man?

5. Would David make a good leader today? Why or why not?

6. What is David's worst crime? His greatest achievement?

7. Which of David's wives do you believe suffered the most at his hands? Did he love Yonatan more than any of them? If so, why might that be?

8. How well does Geraldine Brooks capture David's era and his essence?

9. David is a man driven by passion and violence, but he loves God with equal fervor. How would you explain this?

10. Are you familiar with the psalms attributed to David? If so, do you have a favorite?

11. What might David have done if he had known that Natan was hiding what he knew about his sons' futures? Would David hesitate to kill Natan if he felt the prophet had betrayed him?

12. What is the nature of Natan's feelings toward David? Would you be able to serve a man like him?

13. What is "the secret chord"? Why did Brooks choose this phrase as the novel's title?

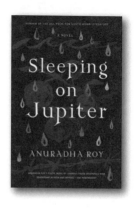

SLEEPING ON JUPITER
Anuradha Roy

A Man Booker Prize–longlisted novel about violence, love, and religion in modern India.

On a train bound for the seaside town of Jarmuli, known for its temples, three elderly women meet a young documentary filmmaker named Nomi, whose braided hair, tattoos, and foreign air set her apart. At a brief stop en route, the women are unprepared to witness a sudden assault on Nomi that leaves her stranded as the train pulls away.

Later in Jarmuli, among pilgrims, priests, and ashrams, the three women disembark only to find that Nomi has managed to arrive on her own. What is someone like her, clearly not a worshipper, doing in this remote place? Over the next five days, the three women live out their long-planned dream of a holiday together; their temple guide pursues a forbidden love; and Nomi is joined by a photographer to scout locations for a documentary. As their lives overlap and collide, Nomi's past comes into focus, and the serene surface of the town is punctured by violence and abuse as Jarmuli is revealed as a place with a long, dark history that transforms all who encounter it. A haunting, vibrant novel that won the DSC Prize for South Asian Literature, *Sleeping on Jupiter* is a brilliantly told story of contemporary India from an internationally acclaimed writer.

*"Anuradha Roy's poetic work of luminous prose deserves a wide readership in India and beyond." —**The Independent***

"Anuradha Roy's deft, empathetic, glowingly intelligent Sleeping on Jupiter *brings a group of characters vividly, radiantly to life. Each seems closed-off into her or his own world, yet they're connected with the lightest, surest of touches. This is storytelling of transcendent depth." —***Rick Simonson, Elliott Bay Book Company, Seattle, WA**

ABOUT THE AUTHOR: **Anuradha Roy** is the author of *The Folded Earth*, which won the *Economist* Crossword Prize, and *An Atlas of Impossible Longing*, which was named a best book of the year by the *Washington Post* and the *Seattle Times*. She lives in Ranikhet, India.

September 2016 | Paperback | Fiction | 264 pp | $16.00 | ISBN 9781555977511
Graywolf Press | Graywolfpress.org | AnuradhaRoy.blogspot.com

CONVERSATION STARTERS

1. *Sleeping on Jupiter* alternates between Nomi's memories and the intersecting paths of the characters in Jarmuli. How does this shifting viewpoint and nonlinear structure inform and strengthen the novel?

2. Throughout the novel, Nomi has a profound effect on the people she encounters. How does her physical appearance challenge expectations and conventions? How does her experience as someone who is both of Jarmuli and marked as a foreigner put her in a unique position?

3. The friendship between Gouri, Latika, and Vidya is a mixture of familiarity, judgment, and affection built up over decades. How do the different life experiences of these women shape what this trip means to each of them? How does this trip change them, both as individuals and as a group?

4. Roy depicts violence in different ways throughout the book. How does the portrayal of Suraj's attack against Nomi at the end of the book differ from Nomi's accounts of war coming to her village and of Guruji's abuse at the ashram? Does the quieter narrative of the friends' holiday provide a respite from the moments of violence, or does it accentuate them?

5. How are the lives of Nomi and Gouri deepened by their respective memories? Which character in the novel focuses repeatedly on the positive aspects of forgetting?

6. Can you name three instances in which water plays a key role in the narrative? What does this imagery evoke for Nomi as it occurs at different points in her life?

7. The temple guide Badal's demeanor with clients contrasts sharply with his interactions with Raghu. Do you think one of these personas is real, and one is artificial? Are there any characters in the book who are not hiding anything?

8. Religion, faith, and devotion play a major role in *Sleeping on Jupiter*. What role does religion have in the lives of the three friends on vacation? What are the points in the novel where faith and devotion occur entirely outside a religious context?

9. The title comes from a passage in which Badal fantasizes about escaping to a distant planet (213–214). Is this fantasy hopeful or devastating? Are there other moments in the novel in which characters look toward the cosmos for connection and a sense of well-being?

THE SUNLIT NIGHT
Rebecca Dinerstein

In the beautiful landscape of the Far North, under the ever-present midnight sun, Frances and Yasha are surprised to find refuge in each other. Their lives have been upended—Frances has fled heartbreak and claustrophobic Manhattan for an isolated artist colony; Yasha, a Russian immigrant raised in a bakery in Brighton Beach, arrives from Brooklyn to fulfill his beloved father's last wish: to be buried "at the top of the world." They have come to learn how to be alone.

But in Lofoten, ninety-five miles north of the Arctic Circle, they form a bond that offers solace amidst great uncertainty. With nimble and sure-footed prose enriched with humor and warmth, Dinerstein reveals that no matter how far we travel to claim our own territory, it is ultimately love that gives us our place in the world.

"Lyrical as a poem, psychologically rich as a thriller, funny, dark, warm, and as knowing of place as any travel book or memoir, The Sunlit Night *marks the appearance of a brave talent."* —**Jonathan Safran Foer**

"Engaging ... [Dinerstein's] blunt, visual language brings the reader back to the most basic senses ... The Sunlit Night *heralds the beginning of an intriguing career in fiction during which Dinerstein will hopefully continue to take us off the beaten path."* —**Huffington Post**

"Luminous ... Dinerstein brings a contagious wonder to her storytelling." —**Oprah Magazine**

*"*The Sunlit Night *is a rare find: it's a literary love story, but for all its nuance, it still has the ability to make you giddy ... with precision and ease, Dinerstein gives us a love story that's about so much more."* —**Bustle.com**

"[A] poetically written novel ... " —***The New York Post***

"Darkly charming." —***The New Yorker***

ABOUT THE AUTHOR: **Rebecca Dinerstein** is the author of *Lofoten*, a bilingual English-Norwegian collection of poems. She received her B.A. from Yale and her M.F.A. in Fiction from New York University, where she was a Rona Jaffe Graduate Fellow. She lives in Brooklyn.

May 2016 | Paperback | Fiction | 272 pp | $16.00 | ISBN 9781632861146
Bloomsbury USA | Bloomsbury.com | RebeccaDinerstein.com

CONVERSATION STARTERS

1. Why do you think Rebecca Dinerstein chose to introduce us to Frances in the context of her relationship with Robert Mason? How does she see the Masons in comparison with her "desperately artistic" (21) family?

2. Examine the role of landscape in *The Sunlit Night*, from urban to wild, Brooklyn to Borg.

3. Frances says of her family: "The only way we knew how to be was in each other's way" (16). The layout of their apartment certainly reflects this reality, but in what other ways do the members of Frances's family intrude on one another? What seems to be Frances's role in the family, and how does that role affect her?

4. Consider Olyana's first appearance at the bakery. How did your understanding of her reason for being there change over the course of her stay? Yasha reflects on a strong memory of sharing a bar of milk chocolate with his mother. How does this memory—and her recurring association with sweets—set the tone for Olyana's character?

5. Upon meeting Nils, Frances thinks: "Here was mankind in his original state ... in all his innocence" (69). What do you think his impression is of her? Do they see each other clearly? Is Frances right about their "unfulfilled romance" (164)?

6. Consider the use of Norse mythology in *The Sunlit Night*, from the Yggdrasil tree sculpture to Olyana's Valkyrie costume. What links can be made between the real world of the novel and the mythological one Haldor presides over at the Viking Museum?

7. While the first four parts of the novel have places for names, the fifth has a period of time: "The Other Season," during which the narrative jumps swiftly between Frances and Yasha. How did this shift affect your understanding of their relationship and its future? Why was it was important for Yasha to stay in Lofoten for part of "the other season"?

8. A sense of professional failure weighs heavily on Frances's father. "What does it matter if you do what you love, if what you love doesn't matter?" (12), he asks her. What conclusions, if any, does the novel reach about this question, particularly with regard to being an artist?

THE TURNER HOUSE
Angela Flournoy

A National Book Award Finalist

A *New York Times* Notable Book

Named a Best Book of the Year by *O, The Oprah Magazine* • *Entertainment Weekly* • NPR • *Essence* • *Men's Journal* • *Buzzfeed* • Bustle • *Time Out* • *Denver Post* • *Publishers Weekly* • *Kirkus Reviews* • *BookPage* • Literary Hub • Kobo • *The Week*

A major new contribution to the story of the American family, *The Turner House* brings us a colorful brood full of love, pride, and unlikely inheritances. It's a striking examination of the American dream and a celebration of the ways in which our families bring us home.

"*A page-turner. Richly wrought and intimate, vivid dialogue. A-*" —*Entertainment Weekly*

"*Engrossing ... In this assured and memorable novel, [Flournoy] provides the feeling of knowing a family from the inside out, as we would wish to know our own.*" —*The New York Times Book Review*

"*An epic that feels deeply personal ... Flournoy's finely tuned empathy infuses her characters with a radiant humanity.*" —*O, The Oprah Magazine*

ABOUT THE AUTHOR: **Angela Flournoy** is a graduate of the Iowa Writers' Workshop and the University of Southern California. Her fiction has appeared in *The Paris Review*, and she has written for the *New Republic*, the *Los Angeles Review of Books*, and other publications. She has taught writing at the University of Iowa and Trinity Washington University. She was raised by a mother from Los Angeles and a father from Detroit.

April 2016 | Paperback | Fiction | 352 pp | $14.95 | ISBN 9780544705166
Houghton Mifflin Harcourt | hmhco.com | AngelaFlournoy.com

CONVERSATION STARTERS

1. The city of Detroit plays a large role in the way characters see themselves. How does the city itself contribute to the story of the Turner family? Can you imagine a similar story taking place elsewhere, or only in Detroit?

2. Cha-Cha sees himself as the patriarch of the family, but he also has trouble getting his siblings to listen to him. How does Cha-Cha's view of himself as the leader prevent his siblings from trusting or respecting him?

3. In their final meeting, Alice tells Cha-Cha that she thinks his haint has made him feel extraordinary, and that she doesn't think he really wants to let it go. Do you agree with her observation? What might the haint provide to Cha-Cha that he otherwise lacks in his life?

4. Alice describes Cha-Cha as the prime minister of his family, and Viola as the queen; she has the title, but is not concerned with day-to-day governance. What is your impression of Viola when you first meet her in the novel, and how does that impression change over time?

5. As the baby, Lelah thinks she has missed out on many of the best moments and secrets in Turner family history. How might her role as the youngest have contributed to her addiction to gambling? Do you think she has truly turned a corner by the novel's end?

6. Troy is the only sibling not present at the party that takes place at the end of the novel. Did you get the impression that he is on the path to change? Why or why not?

7. Both Francis and Cha-Cha have a precarious relationship with belief, both in religion and the supernatural. How do each character's beliefs shift over time, and what effect do those changes have on their relationship to others?

8. The move from Arkansas to Detroit is very important to Turner family history. How is Francis and Viola's relationship changed by the move? How do the challenges they face in Detroit contribute to the way they raise their children?

9. At its core, do you see the Turners as a strongly bonded family? What does it mean for a family to be bonded, especially when people move further away from one another and start their own families?

THE VERSIONS OF US

Laura Barnett

#1 UK Bestseller

The one thing that's certain is they met on a Cambridge street by chance and felt a connection that would last a lifetime. But as for what happened next ... They fell wildly in love, or went their separate ways. They kissed, or they thought better of it. They married soon after, or were together for a few weeks before splitting up. They grew distracted and disappointed with their daily lives together, or found solace together only after hard years spent apart.

With *The Versions of Us*, Laura Barnett has created a world as magical and affecting as those that captivated readers in *One Day* and *Life After Life*. It is a tale of possibilities and consequences that rings across the shifting decades, from the fifties, sixties, seventies, and on to the present, showing how even the smallest choices can define the course of our lives.

"Barnett's enchanting debut imagines three possible lives, three possible love stories—each with its unique joys and sorrows—demonstrating that life has no perfect path." —People, "**The Best New Books**"

"Versions of Us is smart enough to know that the fantasy of infinite possibility is thrilling—but not nearly as much as the reality of true human connection." —Entertainment Weekly

ABOUT THE AUTHOR: **Laura Barnett** is a writer, journalist, and theater critic. She has been on the staff at *The Guardian* and *The Daily Telegraph*, and is now a freelance arts journalist and features writer working for *The Guardian*, *The Observer*, and *Time Out London*, as well as several other national newspapers and magazines. This is her first novel.

May 2016 | Hardcover | Fiction | 416 pp | $26.00 | ISBN 9780544634244
Houghton Mifflin Harcourt | hmhco.com | hmhbooks.com/versionsofus

CONVERSATION STARTERS

1. Explore presentations of marriage and love in the novel. How are each defined and depicted? Does the book define what a "good" marriage entails or what the best kind of love is?

2. What is the role of art in the book? Which of the characters are artists and why do they undertake their artistic pursuits? What purpose do they find in their art? What obstacles do they face as artists? How does their artwork or role as artist shape and inform their identity?

3. The title of the novel is taken from the name of a triptych painted by Jim. What is the subject of the triptych and why is it significant both to Jim and to those who view it? How might it serve as a major symbol within the novel?

4. Thinking about the various settings of the novel, how do the times and places depicted in the novel mirror or help to reveal major themes of the story?

5. Evaluate the parent-child relationships presented in the book. What do the various relationships share in common? What do they reveal about parenthood when considered collectively? How are the characters in the book shaped and influenced by their own childhoods? How do the relationships they shared with their own parents influence and inform the way that they ultimately choose to raise and interact with their children?

6. What are some of the examples of infidelity in the novel? What causes or motivates the various characters to stray from their partners? How do these infidelities or betrayals impact their lives and the lives of those they are unfaithful to? Are any of the characters rewarded for seeking their own happiness?

7. Discuss how the book creates a dialogue around fate and accident versus choice. How much control do the characters have over their own lives and how much is left to chance?

8. How do the three final chapters work together as a cohesive ending? What final message or messages—or questions—do they seem to impart when considered collectively? Do the last three chapters draw the various pieces of the book into a unified whole or present three contradictory conclusions?

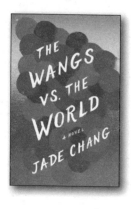

THE WANGS VS. THE WORLD
Jade Chang

One of *Entertainment Weekly*'s Most Anticipated Titles of 2016

Outrageously funny and full of charm, *The Wangs vs. the World* is a debut novel about a wealthy but fractured Chinese immigrant family that had it all, only to lose every last cent—and about the road trip they take across America that binds them back together. It's an entirely fresh look at what it means to belong in America—and how going from glorious riches to (still name-brand) rags brings one family together in a way money never could.

"*Fresh, energetic, and completely hilarious,* The Wangs vs. the World *is my favorite debut of the year.*" —**Jami Attenberg, author of** *Saint Mazie* **and** *The Middlesteins*

"*Funny, brash, honest, full of wit and heart and smarts. This is a novel I wish I could write, have been dying to read, and hope everyone else reads, too.*" —**Charles Yu, author of** *Sorry Please Thank You* **and** *How to Live Safely in a Science Fictional Universe*

"*Jade Chang's debut novel is a heartbreaking, hilarious, and honest American epic: a road trip that's an ultimate escape from our parents' American dream, toward an unknown destination that's both more vulnerable and more hopeful.*" —**J. Ryan Stradal, author of** *Kitchens of the Great Midwest*

ABOUT THE AUTHOR: **Jade Chang** has covered arts and culture as a journalist and editor. She is the recipient of a Sundance Fellowship for Arts Journalism, the AIGA/Winterhouse Award for Design Criticism, and the James D. Houston Memorial scholarship from the Squaw Valley Community of Writers.

October 2016 | Hardcover | Fiction | 368 pp | $26.00 | ISBN 9780544734098
Houghton Mifflin Harcourt | hmhco.com | TheWangs.com

CONVERSATION STARTERS

1. Why is Charles Wang mad at America and mad at history? What does the novel suggest or reveal about "the American Dream"? What does Charles have to say about the American Dream and whom it belongs to?

2. What does Charles hope to recover? Is his plan reasonable—or successful? What do his children and his wife think of his plan?

3. Why did Saina want to be an artist as a young girl? What does she believe the purpose of art should be? What was Saina taught about the choice between art and marriage or motherhood, and what does she come to think of this teaching as an adult?

4. When Andrew turns to comedy, what does he discover as one of the true joys of this kind of performance?

5. Explore the theme of luck in the novel. How much control do the characters seem to have over their own lives, and how much is a matter of luck or fate? How are wealth and good fortune ultimately defined by the story's conclusion?

6. How does each of the characters respond to the loss of the family fortune? Why does Barbra believe that her experience of this loss is different than everyone else's? Who does she believe is most imprisoned by their possessions, and to whom does she think wealth should belong? Do you agree with her? Why or why not?

7. Why does the car accident have such a profound impact on Grace? Do you think she would have had a similar revelation on her own? And how does it relate to Andrew's thoughts about connection and love?

8. At the end of his affair with Dorrie, what does Andrew think is the only thing that matters? Does the rest of the novel seem to support or overturn his point of view? Explain.

9. Explore the treatment of gender in the book. What does Charles believe are the fundamental differences between men and women? Is there any difference in the way that Charles treats his son versus his daughters? How are the female characters in the novel treated by others? Do the female characters seem to have the same opportunities available to them as the men? Discuss.

10. How are the Wangs ultimately affected by their travels together and their reunion?

WE ARE UNPREPARED
Meg Little Reilly

This is a novel about the superstorm that threatens to destroy a marriage, a town and the entire Eastern seaboard. But the destruction begins early, when fear infects people's lives and spreads like the plague.

Ash and Pia move from hipster Brooklyn to rustic Vermont in search of a more authentic life. But just months after settling in, the forecast of a superstorm disrupts their dream. Fear of an impending disaster splits their tight-knit community and exposes the cracks in their marriage. Where Isole was once a place of old farm families, rednecks and transplants, it now divides into paranoid preppers, religious fanatics and government tools, each at odds about what course to take.

We Are Unprepared is an emotional journey, a terrifying glimpse into the human costs of our changing earth and, ultimately, a cautionary tale of survival and the human spirit.

"Smart, prophetic, heartfelt; We Are Unprepared *is just the book I've been waiting to read—both wake-up call and salve for these uncertain times."* —**Robin MacArthur, author of** *Half Wild*

"I couldn't stop thinking of Shirley Jackson's The Lottery *as I read Meg Little Reilly's* We Are Unprepared. *Part environmental thriller, part exploration of marriage, it reveals the psychological storm that lies underneath the tranquil New England façade ready to sweep us into tribal life."* —**Joseph Monninger, award-winning author of** *Eternal on the Water*

"This intimate, well-crafted book is an important addition." —**Charlene D'Avanzo, author of** *Cold Blood, Hot Sea*

"Cli-fi novels don't get much better than this." —**Dan Bloom, The Cli-Fi Report**

ABOUT THE AUTHOR: **Meg Little Reilly** grew up in the offbeat hamlet of Brattleboro, Vermont, where she fantasized about writing novels from a cabin in the woods. After an exciting detour in national politics, she's still working on that plan. She currently lives in the Boston area with her husband, Daniel, and their two daughters. *We Are Unprepared* is her debut novel.

August 2016 | Paperback | Fiction | 368 pp | $15.99 | ISBN 9780778319436
MIRA Books | MIRABooks.com | MegLittleReilly.com

CONVERSATION STARTERS

1. Ash and Pia are chasing a romanticized idea of a more simple and sustainable life. Is this relatable to you, or do you consider it a misguided or perhaps even a privileged fantasy?

2. Do you think Ash and Pia would have made it as a couple in Vermont even if the superstorm had not happened? Why?

3. Which of the characters in *We Are Unprepared* do you consider to be "normal," and which do you think of as "crazy?" Can extreme circumstances make sane people insane?

4. Which of the characters in the novel would you most behave like in these circumstances?

5. If you were facing the same weather disaster, would you align with the civic-minded mayor and Ash, or the prepper group and Pia?

6. Once the storm hits, civil society falls apart quickly, and the death toll begins to mount. Does this seem like hyperbole to you? Do you think local, state and federal governments are this unprepared for a superstorm?

7. Is it noble or selfish for Ash to want to adopt August? Does the lack of choices in a rural, devastated place change this calculation?

8. Fear drives characters in this story to religion, alcohol and guns. What other vices and comforts do we all turn to in anxious times?

9. Does the superstorm seem plausible here? Do you consider it science fiction or an inevitability in our future?

10. No explicit assertion is made in the novel that the changing weather patterns are caused by human behavior, though it's certainly implied. Do you perceive this story to be about man-made climate change or about chance? How might those different positions affect your opinion of the book?

11. In your own life, what aspect of the natural world do you feel most protective of? Is there a place or an experience that you want to shield from the effects of climate change?

12. Do you believe successive generations will have a different relationship to the natural world?

13. Do you believe fiction and art can influence public attitudes about climate change?

NONFICTION

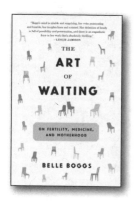

THE ART OF WAITING: ON FERTILITY, MEDICINE, AND MOTHERHOOD
Belle Boggs

A brilliant cultural and personal exploration of the natural, medical, psychological, and political facets of fertility.

In *The Art of Waiting*, Belle Boggs eloquently recounts her realization that she might never be able to conceive. She searches the apparently fertile world around her—the emergence of thirteen-year cicadas, the birth of eaglets near her rural home, and an unusual gorilla pregnancy at a local zoo—for signs that she is not alone. Boggs also explores other aspects of fertility and infertility: the way longing for a child plays out in the classic Coen brothers film *Raising Arizona*; the depiction of childlessness in literature, from *Macbeth* to *Who's Afraid of Virginia Woolf?*; the financial and legal complications that accompany alternative means of family making; the expressions of iconic writers grappling with motherhood and fertility. She reports, with great empathy, complex stories of couples who adopted domestically and from overseas, LGBT couples considering assisted reproduction and surrogacy, and women and men reflecting on childless or childfree lives.

Boggs distills her time of waiting into an expansive contemplation of fertility, choice, and the many possible roads to making a life and making a family.

"In this profound, deeply moving study of fertility and motherhood, Belle Boggs takes us on a remarkable journey. Her book ponders the nature of reproduction in modern America, which is of necessity a means of pondering the nature of family, which is in turn a means of pondering the nature of intimacy and love." —**Andrew Solomon**

"In this lovely meditation, Belle Boggs explores a landscape suddenly illuminated by the bright light of her own uncertain future ... What The Art of Waiting *suggests to me is that all our moments that feel fruitless may be bearing their own sort of fruit, in their own time."* —**Eula Biss**

ABOUT THE AUTHOR: **Belle Boggs** is the author of *Mattaponi Queen*. Her work has appeared in *Orion*, *Harper's*, the *Paris Review*, *Ecotone*, *Slate*, and elsewhere. She lives in North Carolina.

Sept 2016 | Paperback | Nonfiction | 242 pp | $16.00 | ISBN 9781555977498
Graywolf Press | GraywolfPress.org | BelleBoggs.com

CONVERSATION STARTERS

1. How do you define the words "family" and "parent"?

2. How do ideas about luck, fate, and "nature" influence our perceptions about a person's ability to have a child?

3. *The Art of Waiting* looks at other cultural and literary representations of infertility and childlessness, including *Macbeth*, *Who's Afraid of Virginia Woolf?*, and the Coen brothers film *Raising Arizona*. Are you familiar with any of these examples, and if so, did *The Art of Waiting* change your perception of these works? Can you think of other cultural narratives that portray infertility or childlessness?

4. It is often incorrectly assumed that the majority of infertility patients are older, highly educated, wealthy white women. How do these misconceptions connect to larger problems of racial and social inequity? What unique obstacles do LGBT people face when trying to start a family?

5. How has scientists' understanding of the term "biological" changed, and what does that mean for adoptive families and families created using donor eggs, sperm, or embryos?

6. How can Assisted Reproductive Technology be seen as empowering?

7. According to Boggs's research, how does the health insurance industry influence whether Assistive Reproductive Technology is a viable option?

8. Why do you think Boggs uses examples of reproductive stories from other species, such as the lowland gorillas at the North Carolina Zoo, to frame the story of human reproductive longing?

9. It is clear early on in the book that Boggs's story will include the birth of her daughter, but the broader narrative of the book includes the other paths she could have taken and the outcomes she could have experienced. How do you think your experience of the book would have changed if Boggs had decided to focus only on her personal narrative? How do you think your experience would have been different if this memoir aspect was omitted?

10. On one level the book's title is a literal reference to the patience required for anyone hoping to become a parent. How does "*The Art of Waiting*" evoke an even deeper philosophical meaning?

BODY OF WATER: A SAGE, A SEEKER, AND THE WORLD'S MOST ALLURING FISH
Chris Dombrowski

Chris Dombrowski was playing a numbers game: two passions—poetry and fly-fishing; two children, one of them in utero; and an income hovering perilously close to zero. Enter, at this particularly challenging moment, a miraculous email: *can't go, it's all paid for, just book a flight to Miami.*

Thus began a journey that would lead to the Bahamas and to David Pinder, a legendary bonefishing guide. Bonefish are prized for their elusiveness and their tenacity. And no one was better at hunting them than Pinder, a Bahamian whose accuracy and patience were virtuosic. *He knows what the fish think*, said one fisherman, *before they think it.*

By the time Dombrowski meets Pinder, however, he has been abandoned by the industry he helped build. With cataracts from a lifetime of staring at the water and a tiny severance package after forty years of service, he watches as the world of his beloved bonefish is degraded by tourists he himself did so much to attract. But as Pinder's stories unfold, Dombrowski discovers a profound integrity and wisdom in the guide's life.

"A brilliant book. Destined to be a classic." —**Jim Harrison**

"Via the hearts of two men utterly in love with the wounded world in which their calling takes place, Body of Water *pours forth beauties, subtleties, dark history, and insight with an unforced lyrical power I associate with no lesser word than 'masterpiece.' Dombrowski's Michigan-to-Montana trajectory updates Jim Harrison, his comedic fishing scenes bear comparison to Thomas McGuane, and his powers of ebullient reflection bring to mind Mary Oliver— yet I've read no book anything like* Body of Water, *and enjoyed no book in memory more."* —**David James Duncan**

ABOUT THE AUTHOR: Born in Michigan, **Chris Dombrowski** earned his MFA from the University of Montana. He is the author of two collections of poems, and his poetry and nonfiction have been widely published. Also a fly-fishing guide, Dombrowski lives in Missoula, Montana.

October 2016 | Hardcover | Nonfiction | 232 pp | $18.00 | ISBN 9781571313522
Milkweed Editions | Milkweed.org

CONVERSATION STARTERS

1. Why did Dombrowski name the book *Body of Water*? What different roles and significances does water have throughout the text?

2. David Pinder Sr. is described as "legendary." Why is this word more apt than famous to describe the elder guide?

3. The value of local knowledge is an important thread in this book. What local knowledge do you have? And how would you share it with someone else?

4. Dombrowski describes hunting in this book as a dedication "to the occupation of being creaturely" (171-172). How would you define "being creaturely"?

5. Guiding, specifically guiding fishing trips, is considered from a number of different perspectives in this book. What does it mean to be a guide?

6. Two types of conservation are described in this book, one led by wealthy organizations and individuals, and another led by local citizens. Which do you think has more potential for long-term success?

7. Fishing is an occupation, a vocation, and a sport in *Body of Water*. Is there something in your life that operates similarly to the way angling does for Dombrowski?

8. Ecotourism is the backbone of the Bahamian economy. How does this growing form of travel benefit or imperil smaller countries?

9. David Pinder Sr. is both deeply spiritual and deeply religious. How do these characteristics inform his life?

CAN'T WE TALK ABOUT SOMETHING MORE PLEASANT?: A MEMOIR
Roz Chast

#1 *New York Times* **Bestseller**

2014 National Book Award Finalist

Winner of: 2014 Kirkus Prize in Nonfiction, National Book Critics Circle Award, 2014 Books for a Better Life Award, 2015 National Cartoonists Society Reuben Award

In her first memoir, Roz Chast brings her signature wit to the topic of aging parents. Spanning the last several years of their lives and told through four-color cartoons, family photos, and documents, and a narrative as rife with laughs as it is with tears, Chast's memoir is both comfort and comic relief for anyone experiencing the life-altering loss of elderly parents.

While the particulars are Chast-ian in their idiosyncrasies—an anxious father who had relied heavily on his wife for stability as he slipped into dementia and a former assistant principal mother whose overbearing personality had sidelined Roz for decades—the themes are universal: adult children accepting a parental role; aging and unstable parents leaving a family home for an institution; dealing with uncomfortable physical intimacies; and hiring strangers to provide the most personal care.

"Funny and smart, of course, but also bravely self-revealing and sad ... " —*Newsday*

"Both moving and darkly funny." —*The Washington Post*

"Roz Chast's inspired graphic memoir is a tour de force of dark humor and illuminating pathos about her parents' final years as only this quirky genius of pen and ink could construe them." —*Elle*

"Chast's book is deliciously funny and, at the same time, sober and true." —*New Republic*

ABOUT THE AUTHOR: **Roz Chast** grew up in Brooklyn. Her cartoons began appearing in *The New Yorker* in 1978. Since then, she has published more than one thousand cartoons in the magazine. She has written and illustrated many books, including *What I Hate: From A to Z,* and the collections of her own cartoons *The Party After You Left* and *Theories of Everything.*

Sept 2016 | Paperback | Nonfiction | 240 pp | $19.00 | ISBN 9781632861016
Bloomsbury USA | Bloomsbury.com | RozChast.com

CONVERSATION STARTERS

1. Have you had a similar discussion with your parents and/or children about aging and long-term care plans? What was the result? At what age do you think parents and children should have this conversation?

2. Which part(s) of the book, if any, could you relate to the most? Did you find yourself empathizing more with George and Elizabeth, or Roz? Did this change as you progressed through the book?

3. Which aspects of the role reversal Chast depicts—the child assuming a caretaker role—were the most striking to you? What emotions did you experience as you were reading about the challenges Roz, George, and Elizabeth all faced?

4. Whose experience is more frightening to you—George and Elizabeth's, or Roz's?

5. Which parts of the memoir made you laugh? Which made you cry? Did Chast's use of humor surprise you? Do you think it's necessary or inappropriate to approach this type of subject with humor?

6. Did your perceptions of George and Elizabeth as parents, spouses, and people in general change as the book went on? If so, in what ways?

7. In your opinion, what is the greatest loss that George and Elizabeth experience as they age?

8. Have you considered your own end-of-life plans? Why or why not? Was the book informational for you, and if so, what did you learn? Has reading this book changed your thinking about your own end-of-life care?

9. What is your opinion of Roz's decision to keep her parents' ashes in her closet?

10. Chast discusses at length her complicated feelings regarding her mother, and how her relationship with her mother differed greatly from the one she had with her father. Do you think this has an impact on Roz's approach to her parents' end-of-life care? Do you think Elizabeth was a good mother? Do you think Roz was a good daughter?

11. Toward the end of the book, Roz struggles with the financial cost of her mother's care, compounded by the fact that she's "not living and not dying." What are your views regarding this hardship, and her mother's condition?

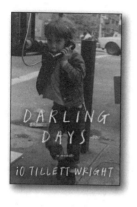

DARLING DAYS: A MEMOIR
iO Tillett Wright

Born into the beautiful bedlam of downtown New York in the eighties, iO Tillett Wright came of age at the intersection of punk, poverty, heroin, and art. *Darling Days* is a provocative examination of culture and identity, of the instincts that shape us and the norms that deform us, and of the courage and resilience it takes to listen closely to your deepest self. When a group of boys refuse to let six-year-old, female-born iO play ball, iO instantly adopts a new persona, becoming a boy named Ricky. It is the start of a profound exploration of gender and identity through the tenderest years. Alternating between the harrowing and the hilarious, *Darling Days* is the candid, tough, and stirring memoir of a young person in search of an authentic self.

"An earnest and heartfelt memoir cloaked under a battle-toughened exterior."
—**Kirkus Reviews**

"It's already a rare and wonderful thing to have a great story-but a unique and compelling voice to tell it with is even rarer ... A terrific, terrific book."
—**Anthony Bourdain**

"Reading Darling Days *I'm reminded of what I liked best in Patti Smith's* Just Kids. *In brutally honest and passionate prose, iO presents the blossoming of an artist, this time in the eighties, on New York's Lower East Side."* —**Mitchell Kaplan, Books and Books**

"iO Tillett Wright is nothing short of a force of nature—an artist, an activist, and a survivor. iO has packed a lot in her young years and in this extraordinary memoir has created something brave and true, as devastating as it is inspiring." —**Jill Soloway, Emmy-award winning creator of** *Transparent*

ABOUT THE AUTHOR: **iO Tillett Wright** is an artist, activist, actor, speaker, TV host and writer. iO's work deals with identity, be it through photography and the Self Evident Truths Project/We Are You campaign or on television as the co-host of MTV's *Suspect*. iO has exhibited artwork in New York and Tokyo, was a featured contributor on Underground Culture to T: *The New York Times Style Magazine*, and has had photography featured in *GQ*, *Elle*, *New York Magazine*, and *The New York Times Magazine*. iO is also a regular speaker at universities. A native New Yorker, iO is now based in Los Angeles.

September 2016 | Hardcover | Nonfiction | 400 pp | $26.99 | ISBN 9780062368201
Ecco | HarperCollins.com | DarlingDays.com

CONVERSATION STARTERS

1. iO's Ma is a dominating figure in the book—a character with many shades. How did iO present Ma here? Did your opinion and perception of her change throughout the book?

2. iO grew up in troubled circumstances and struggled significantly to meet basic needs. What resources or strategies do you see iO develop in order to cope with these circumstances?

3. Discuss your feelings about the ethics of memoir-writing. Would you ever write about your family and, if so, would you try to publish the work? Would you allow your relatives to read your memoir before it was published?

4. The obligations owed to family members is a powerful recurring theme throughout the memoir. How did you feel that various family members—and iO—lived up to or failed to live up to these obligations? And what challenges of being a parent, and of being a child, were highlighted here?

5. How would you describe iO's journey of navigating gender and sexuality? How central was this element of the memoir for you?

6. Discuss the role of self-presentation in the book, of one's public versus private image. Which characters brought this difference to life for you most powerfully?

7. Which of iO's relationships and friendships had the most impact for you as a reader and what did you take from them?

8. Try to imagine the author's process of re-creating these distinct periods from the past, especially those from early childhood. How would you go about undertaking this task of imaginative re-creation if you were faced with it? How reliable is one's memory of events from childhood?

9. Discuss the role of setting and place and, especially, the Lower East Side in the nineties. What did iO do to render a vibrant sense of place—what details or anecdotes particularly captured the scene for you?

10. *Darling Days* is explicitly compared to *Just Kids* in one of the comments on the book's jacket. If you've read that book, how apt do you think that comparison is? If you haven't read that book, what other memoirs would you compare *Darling Days* to?

IS IT ALL IN YOUR HEAD?: TRUE STORIES OF IMAGINARY ILLNESS

Suzanne O'Sullivan, MD

Winner of the 2016 Wellcome Prize, a neurologist's insightful and compassionate look into the misunderstood world of psychosomatic disorders, told through individual case histories

It's happened to all of us: our cheeks flush red when we say the wrong thing, or our hearts skip a beat when a certain someone walks by. But few of us realize how much more dramatic and extreme our bodies' reactions to emotions can be. Many people who see their doctor have medically unexplained symptoms, and in the vast majority of these cases, a psychosomatic cause is suspected. And yet, the diagnosis of a psychosomatic disorder can make a patient feel dismissed as a hypochondriac, a faker, or just plain crazy.

In *Is It All in Your Head?* neurologist Suzanne O'Sullivan, MD, takes us on a journey through the world of psychosomatic illness, where we meet patients such as Rachel, a promising young dancer now housebound by chronic fatigue syndrome, and Mary, whose memory loss may be her mind's way of protecting her from remembering her husband's abuse. O'Sullivan reveals the hidden stresses behind their mysterious symptoms, approaching a sensitive topic with patience and understanding. She addresses the taboos surrounding psychosomatic disorders, teaching us that "it's all in your head" doesn't mean that something isn't real.

"Doctors' tales of their patients' weirder afflictions have been popular since Oliver Sacks ... Few of them, however, are as bizarre or unsettling as those described in this extraordinary and extraordinarily compassionate book."
—James McConnachie, *Sunday Times*

ABOUT THE AUTHOR: **Suzanne O'Sullivan, MD,** has been a consultant in neurology since 2004, working first at The Royal London Hospital and currently as a consultant in clinical neurophysiology and neurology at The National Hospital for Neurology and Neurosurgery. She has developed an expertise in working with patients with psychogenic disorders, alongside her work with those suffering from physical diseases, such as epilepsy.

January 2017 | Hardcover | Nonfiction | 352 pp | $26.95 | ISBN 9781590517956
Other Press | OtherPress.com

CONVERSATION STARTERS

1. Before reading *Is It All in Your Head?*, did you know anything about psychogenic disorders, or about physical responses to emotional stimuli more generally? What did you learn that you didn't know before? What surprised you?

2. O'Sullivan emphasizes the importance of *believing* her patients—of acknowledging that their physical pain is in fact real, even though she believes it to have a psychological origin. Do you believe them? If you were in O'Sullivan's place, what would it take to convince you that your patient isn't "faking it"?

3. Even after rigorous medical testing, most of O'Sullivan's patients are initially reluctant to accept her diagnosis of a psychogenic disorder. Why do you think that is? How do you think you would react to such a diagnosis?

4. Have you ever experienced a psychosomatic illness or affliction? How did you know that it was mental rather than physical?

5. What did you think of O'Sullivan's relationship with her patients? Does her experience and understanding of psychogenic disorders make it easier or harder for them to accept her diagnoses?

6. Were there any particular patients in *Is It All in Your Head?* that you could relate to? Who? Why?

7. The absence of a definitive medical cause of illness or pain does not prove that it is "all in your head." If you were one of O'Sullivan's patients, what would it take to convince you that your symptoms might stem from psychological trauma rather than physical trauma?

8. Do you agree with O'Sullivan that a stigma exists against sufferers of psychogenic illness or pain? Has reading *Is It All in Your Head?* changed the way you think about these disorders and those who suffer from them?

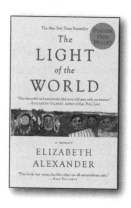

THE LIGHT OF THE WORLD: A MEMOIR
Elizabeth Alexander

A *New York Times* bestseller, a Pulitzer Prize Finalist, a National Book Critics Circle Finalist, a Books for a Better Life Award Finalist, and an NAACP Award Finalist

In *The Light of the World*, Elizabeth Alexander finds herself at an existential crossroads after the sudden death of her husband. Reflecting with gratitude on the exquisite beauty of the intimacy they shared, grappling with the resulting void, and finding solace in caring for her two teenage sons, Alexander channels her poetic sensibilities into rich, lucid prose that universalizes a very personal quest for meaning and acceptance in the wake of loss. *The Light of the World* is both an endlessly compelling memoir and a deeply felt meditation on the blessings of love, family, art, and community. For those who have loved and lost, or for anyone who cares about what matters most, this book is required reading.

"Both raw and exquisitely crafted, mercilessly direct and sometimes lavishly metaphorical ... The Light of the World is, quite simply, a miracle."
—*The Boston Sunday Globe*

"It's magnificent." —**First Lady Michelle Obama**

"A gorgeous and intimate tribute" —*Newsday*

ABOUT THE AUTHOR: **Elizabeth Alexander** composed and recited "Praise Song for the Day" for President Barack Obama's 2009 inauguration. She is the author of six books of poetry—including *American Sublime*, a finalist for the Pulitzer Prize—and is the first winner of the Jackson Prize for Poetry and a National Endowment for the Arts and Guggenheim fellow. She is the Frederick Iseman Professor of Poetry at Yale University.

September 2016 | Paperback | Nonfiction | 240 pp | $15.99 | ISBN 9781455599868
Grand Central Publishing | GrandCentralPublishing.com | ElizabethAlexander.net

CONVERSATION STARTERS

1. Consider the title of the book, which is taken from a poem by Derek Walcott: "O Beauty, you are the light of the world!". What did you think about it before you read the memoir? What do you think now?

2. In particular, address the question of self-pity. Does Alexander pity herself? In what ways does she indulge that impulse, and in what ways does she deny it?

3. Read the Jeannette Walls blurb at the beginning of the book. Why do you suppose she describes *The Light of the World* as a "book about the redemptive realization that such pain is a small price to pay for such love?"

4. Discuss the notion of what it means to grieve in the absence of religious culture. Have you ever searched for meaning after a loss, where none initially presented itself? How did it hinder or help your healing?

5. Consider Alexander's use of time throughout the book. How did it help structure the story and how did it affect your reading experience?

6. Before *The Light of the World*, had you ever read any of Elizabeth Alexander's poetry? Are there passages in which her poetic attention to word, rhythm, and musicality are particularly evident?

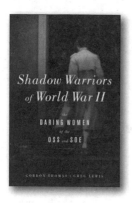

SHADOW WARRIORS OF WORLD WAR II: THE DARING WOMEN OF THE OSS AND SOE

Gordon Thomas and Greg Lewis

"I hate wars and violence, but if they come then I don't see why we women should just wave a proud good-bye and then knit them balaclavas." —Nancy Wake, SOE agent

"I discovered how easy it was to make highly trained, professionally closemouthed patriots give away their secrets in bed." —Betty Pack, agent with the British Secret Intelligence Service and the Office of Strategic Services

In a dramatically different tale of espionage and conspiracy in World War II, *Shadow Warriors of World War II* unveils the history of the courageous women who volunteered to work behind enemy lines.

Sent into Nazi-occupied Europe by the United States' Office of Strategic Services (OSS) and Britain's Special Operations Executive (SOE), these women helped establish a web of resistance groups across the continent. Their heroism, initiative, and resourcefulness contributed to the Allied breakout of the Normandy beachheads and even infiltrated Nazi Germany at the height of the war, into the very heart of Hitler's citadel—Berlin. Young and daring, the female agents accepted that they could be captured, tortured, or killed, but others were always ready to take their place. Women of enormous cunning and strength of will, the Shadow Warriors' stories have remained largely untold until now.

ABOUT THE AUTHORS: **Gordon Thomas** is the author of *Gideon's Spies* and *Operation Exodus*, and the recipient of two Mark Twain Society Awards, an Edgar Award, and the Citizens Commission for Human Rights Lifetime Achievement Award for Investigative Journalism.

Greg Lewis is a journalist, BAFTA–award-winning–producer, and author of several books, including *A Bullet Saved My Life* and *The Death of Justice*.

January 2017 | Hardcover | Nonfiction | 304 pp | $26.99 | ISBN 9781613730867
Chicago Review Press | ChicagoReviewPress.com

CONVERSATION STARTERS

1. *Shadow Warriors* describes how in World War II women were trained as spies on a large scale for the first time. What advantages did the Allied intelligence services believe female agents had over men?

2. Betty Pack used her sexuality to gain men's trust and obtain information for the British and Americans. Discuss how she viewed espionage and extra marital affairs. In what ways did she see both deceptions as the same? In what ways did she see her way of spying as different from those who carried a gun?

3. Wireless operator Yvonne Cormeau learned that she should not wear a watch while posing as a farmer's wife, as French peasants did not wear one. What else did the women learn about disguising themselves behind enemy lines?

4. Virginia Hall was one of the Allies' most successful agents in occupied France, even though she had lost part of her leg in an accident before the war. How did she did use her work as a journalist to help her as a spy? What changed for her after America entered the war?

5. Why was life for a female wireless operator particularly dangerous? What did people like Yvonne Cormeau do to reduce their chances of capture?

6. When Elizabeth Devereaux Rochester arrived in France she appealed for weapons to be sent to the French resistance. British intelligence immediately picked her to return to occupied France and she was delighted. Why do you think this was? Why do you think she was eager to return?

7. Why do you think SOE officers were reluctant to believe that some of their radio operators had been captured? As the intelligence networks grew and more agents arrived in France security became more difficult. Why was that?

8. Odette Sansom felt a fear that "anything could happen at anytime." What were the most difficult things about spying behind enemy lines? How would you cope with leading a double life?

9. When Pearl Witherington was offered a medal for civilian work she returned it. She said her work was of a "purely military nature." What do you think about the way the women were treated by the authorities after the war?

A WOMAN ON THE EDGE OF TIME: A SON INVESTIGATES HIS TRAILBLAZING MOTHER'S YOUNG SUICIDE

Jeremy Gavron

An *Observer* book of the year

In London, 1965, a brilliant young woman—a prescient advocate for women's rights—has just gassed herself to death, leaving behind a suicide note, two young sons, and a soon-to-be-published book: *The Captive Wife*. No one had ever imagined that Hannah Gavron might take her own life. Beautiful, sophisticated, and swept up in the progressive '60s, she was a promising academic and the wife of a rising entrepreneur. But there was another side to Hannah, as Jeremy Gavron reveals in this searching portrait of his mother.

Gavron—who was four when his mother killed herself—attempts to piece her life together from letters, diaries, photos, and memories of old acquaintances. Ultimately, he not only uncovers Hannah's struggle to carve out a place in a man's world; he examines the suffocating constrictions placed on every ambitious woman in the mid-twentieth century.

"Beautifully written—wholly unique—[it] is an elegy/memoir that is also a kind of detective story—in which the author investigates, with as much dread as hope, the circumstances leading to the suicide of his charismatic and accomplished mother many years before. It is difficult not to rush through Gavron's compelling story." —**Joyce Carol Oates**

"Gavron's quest to find his mother has produced a groundbreaking book and moving portrait of a spirited young woman—a 'captive wife'—who refused to accept the social constraints of her time. Unforgettable." —**Tina Brown**

"This pioneering, intense and visceral work ... is both an act of mourning and a revelation of life. The genius of A Woman on the Edge of Time *is that the impossible, very real Hannah Gavron—cheeky, warm, clever, determined, brilliant, shining, paradoxical—comes so fully back to life."* —**Ali Smith**, *Times Literary Supplement*

ABOUT THE AUTHOR: **Jeremy Gavron** is the author of *The Book of Israel*, winner of the Encore Award, and *An Acre of Barren Ground*. A former foreign correspondent in Africa and Asia, he now lives in London, and teaches in the MFA program at Warren Wilson College in NC.

September 2016 | Hardcover | Nonfiction | 272 pp | $24.95 | ISBN 9781615193387
The Experiment | TheExperimentPublishing.com

CONVERSATION STARTERS

1. Joyce Carol Oates calls this book an "elegy/memoir that is also a kind of detective story." Which passages in this book read most like mystery? Do you think the book reveals more about Hannah or Jeremy? Why?

2. In the book, a fellow sociologist of Hannah's says that "to succeed in those days women had to give up something—children, work, femininity—whereas Hannah wanted and appeared able to have everything" (3). To what extent did Hannah have "everything"? Do you think children, work, and femininity constituted everything for her? If not, what else might she have prized, and what might she have considered missing from her life?

3. Woven into the book are excerpts of Hannah's letters. How does hearing from Hannah herself affect how you view her?

4. Reading through Hannah's early report cards, Jeremy writes: "I don't doubt that she was assertive, boisterous, noisy, but I wonder if there would have been so much concern about these characteristics if she had been a boy" (73). How, if at all, would these gender perceptions have changed today? Do any of the men in Hannah's life treat her as an equal? Would Hannah's life have turned out differently if she lived even a few years later? If so, how? What if she were a young woman today?

5. "For as long as I can remember," Jeremy writes, "my father's gaze has been directed at what lies ahead. He doesn't believe in worrying about the past, or lingering over problems that can't be solved" (158). In what ways has Jeremy's father's disinclination to revisit the past shaped the way this story unfolds?

6. "Guilt is one of the most devastating legacies of suicide," Jeremy writes (166). What legacies did Hannah leave behind?

7. The epigraph of this book comes from the writer Amos Oz, and reads: "Have I betrayed them all again by telling the story? Or is it the other way round: would I have betrayed them if I had not told it?" Do you find Jeremy's story, in which he writes so intimately about his mother's life, at all a betrayal? Why or why not?

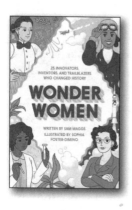

WONDER WOMEN: 25 INNOVATORS, INVENTORS, AND TRAILBLAZERS WHO CHANGED HISTORY

Sam Maggs

Smart women have always been able to achieve amazing things, even when the odds have been stacked against them. In *Wonder Women*, author Sam Maggs tells the stories of the brilliant, brainy, and totally rad women who broke barriers as scientists, engineers, mathematicians, doctors, inventors, spies, and more. She also includes interviews with modern-day women in STEM careers, an extensive bibliography, and a guide to women-centric science and technology organizations—all to show the many ways the geeky girls of today can help build the future.

"Whether you want to know about suffragists, awesome historical lady ninjas, or the other butt kicking, trailblazing smarties in between, Wonder Women *will have something for you!"* —**Amy Poehler's Smart Girls**

ABOUT THE AUTHOR: **Sam Maggs** is an assistant writer for BioWare and the best-selling author of *The Fangirl's Guide to the Galaxy* (Quirk Books, 2015). Named "Awesome Geek Feminist of the Year" by Women Write about Comics, Sam received her MA in Victorian literature in 2011 and now appears on TV and movie screens across Canada. She has written for *Marie Claire*, *PC Gamer*, the *Guardian*, *National Post*, the Mary Sue, and more. You can geek out with her about Mass Effect or Jeff Goldblum on Twitter @SamMaggs.

October 2016 | Hardcover | Nonfiction | 240 pp | $16.99 | ISBN 9781594749254
Quirk Books | QuirkBooks.com | SamMaggs.com

CONVERSATION STARTERS

1. In the introduction of *Wonder Women*, Sam Maggs talks about representation. What does representation mean to you? And do you share Maggs's view about the importance of representation in media and in our daily lives?

2. The innovators showcased in *Wonder Women* are diverse, but they also have some important traits in common. What do you think some of their commonalities are?

3. Maggs chose to tell the stories of women who were under-recognized for their achievements. Was there anyone in the book that you already knew of?

4. Which woman's story did you find the most fascinating?

5. Did you read anything in *Wonder Women* that surprised you or that stirred your emotions?

6. What lessons did you take away from the profiles of the modern day women working in STEM?

7. How do you think that you can help to bring better recognition to women in STEM and encourage younger generations to become more active in STEM-related fields?

8. If you had the opportunity to have a dinner party with three of the women profiled in *Wonder Women*, either living or dead, who would you choose? And why?

9. Are there any women that weren't profiled in this book that you think of as wonder women?

YOUNG ADULT

AMERICAN STREET
Ibi Zoboi

On the corner of American Street and Joy Road, Fabiola Toussaint thought she would finally find *une belle vie*—the good life. But after leaving Port au Prince, Haiti, Fabiola's mother is detained by U.S. immigration, leaving Fabiola to navigate her loud, American cousins—Chantal, Donna and Princess—the grittiness of Detroit's Westside, a new school, and a surprising romance, all on her own. Just as she finds her footing in this strange new world, a dangerous proposition presents itself, and Fabiola must learn that freedom comes at a cost. Trapped at the crossroads of an impossible choice, will she pay the price for the American dream?

"A lovely and poignant meditation on one girl's struggle to find her way in a new world." —**Nicola Yoon, bestselling author of** *Everything, Everything*

"Brimming with culture, magic, warmth, and unabashed rawness, American Street *is ultimately a blistering tale of humanity. This is* Manchild in the Promised Land, *for a new generation, and a remarkable debut from Zoboi, who without question is an inevitable force in storytelling."* —**Jason Reynolds, award-winning co-author of** *All American Boys*

"Zoboi's nascent storytelling gifts ensnare from page one. To this spellbinding voice of the next generation, I bow." —**Rita Williams-Garcia,** *The New York Times* **bestselling author and three-time winner of the Coretta Scott King Award**

ABOUT THE AUTHOR: **Ibi Zoboi** is a Pushcart nominated author who was born in Port-au-Prince, Haiti. She now lives in Brooklyn with her husband, and their three young children.

February 2017 | Hardcover | Young Adult | 336 pp | $17.99 | ISBN 9780062473042
Balzer + Bray | HarperCollins.com

CONVERSATION STARTERS

1. How does the author use Creole and American slang throughout the book? What does the use of either or both languages suggest about the characters in the novel?

2. What are some of the similarities between Detroit, Michigan and Port-au-Prince, Haiti? How do they differ?

3. How do you think Fabiola changes over the course of the novel? What were some of the events that facilitated those changes?

4. How would you describe the Three Bees? Which one of their characters would you most identify with and why?

5. What does Fabiola mean when she says "Now I don't look so ... Haitian. So immigrant." How would the Three Bees interpret those words? What are some examples of when Fabiola feels like she isn't only Haitian but she's not fully Americanized either?

6. How did you feel about Kasim when you first met him? Did you trust him? What about Dray? How were Kasim and Dray the same? How were they different?

7. Describe the different forms of fighting that take place throughout the novel. What are the various reasons that the characters are involved in fighting? Do you think they have a choice about if they would want to fight or back down? Why or why not?

8. Describe what happens at the party in Gross Pointe Park. How would you react in that situation? Would you have trusted Detective Stevens? Why or why not?

9. Magical realism combines realistic narrative and naturalistic technique with surreal elements of dream or fantasy. How does this enhance Fabiola's spirituality throughout the book?

10. Explain the significance of this quote: "But then I realize that everyone is climbing their own mountain here in America. They are tall and mighty and they live in the hearts and everyday lives of the people."

THE ART OF HOLDING ON AND LETTING GO

Kristin Bartley Lenz

Junior Library Guild Selection

In her powerful debut, Kristin Bartley Lenz delivers an evocative story of grief, acceptance, and ultimately, self-discovery.

Competitive climber Cara Jenkins feels most at home high off the ground, clinging to a rock wall by her fingertips. She's enjoyed a roaming life with her mountaineering parents, making the natural world her jungle gym, the writings of Annie Dillard and Henry David Thoreau her textbooks. But when tragedy strikes on an Ecuadoran mountaintop, Cara's nomadic lifestyle comes to an abrupt halt.

Starting over at her grandparents' home in suburban Detroit, Cara embarks on a year of discovery, uncovering unknown strengths, friendships, and first love. Cara's journey illustrates the transformative power of nature, love and loss, and discovering that home can be far from where you started.

"Cara is an appealing, engaging narrator. Surrounded by a well-rounded cast, Cara's journey toward a peaceful, fulfilling life is almost perfectly depicted. A compelling, unusual coming-of-age story." —Kirkus Reviews

"Lenz offers a thoughtful meditation on life after loss. Lenz effortlessly explains complicated climbing terminology and intermixes moments of levity with contemplative quotations from naturalists and mountain climbers." —**Publishers Weekly**

"I loved this book. There's plenty of humor, romance, and great rock climbing scenes that will have you riveted." —**Anne Rouyer, New York Public Library**

ABOUT THE AUTHOR: **Kristin Bartley Lenz** is a writer and social worker whose career has taken her through rural Appalachia, the California Bay Area, and inner-city Detroit. She is the co-editor of the Michigan Chapter blog for the Society of Children's Book Writers and Illustrators. *The Art of Holding On and Letting Go* is her first book.

Sept 2016 | Paperback | Young Adult | 306 pp | $12.95 | ISBN 9780996864916
Elephant Rock Books | ElephantRockBooks.com | KristinBartleyLenz.com

CONVERSATION STARTERS

1. How do the writings of naturalists such as John Muir, Henry David Thoreau, and Annie Dillard shape Cara's worldview?

2. Cara is deeply affected by the death of her uncle Max. In what ways does she mourn and celebrate his memory?

3. The contrast between Cara's climbing life and her suburban life are in conflict throughout the novel. How does she make peace with these competing landscapes?

4. Cara feels most free when she's climbing. What activity in your life brings you this kind of joy and liberation?

5. Did you notice the lack of technology in Cara's life? What are the effects of Cara not having her nose buried in a cell phone 24-7? What is she able to experience more fully?

6. How does being an outsider on the climbing team and in school shape Cara's identity?

7. How does Kaitlyn's experience and growth throughout the novel mirror Cara's? How do these friends help each other?

8. How does Cara's relationship with her free-spirited parents evolve over the course of the novel? What does Cara understand about her parents at the end of the book that she didn't at the beginning?

9. Compare and contrast the three different settings of the novel. How do these environments contribute to the action and meaning of the book?

10. Cara spends the first two-thirds of the novel wanting to return to California. What does she realize about the meaning of home during her time with Nick, Kaitlyn, and her grandparents?

BURN BABY BURN

Meg Medina

Nora Lopez is seventeen during the infamous New York summer of 1977, when the city is besieged by arson, a massive blackout, and a serial killer named Son of Sam who shoots young women on the streets. Nora's family life isn't going so well either: her bullying brother, Hector, is growing more threatening by the day, her mother is helpless and falling behind on the rent, and her father calls only on holidays. All Nora wants is to turn eighteen and be on her own. And while there is a cute new guy who started working with her at the deli, is dating even worth the risk when the killer likes picking off couples who stay out too late?

Award-winning author Meg Medina transports us to a time when New York seemed balanced on a knife-edge, with tempers and temperatures running high, to share the story of a young woman who discovers that the greatest dangers are often closer than we like to admit—and the hardest to accept.

"Meg Medina once again shines in evoking a specific setting peopled with complex, diverse characters." —Chicago Tribune

"Rooted firmly in historical events, Medina's latest offers up a uniquely authentic slice-of-life experience set against a hazy, hot, and dangerous NYC backdrop. Rocky and Donna Summer and the thumping beats of disco, as well as other references from the time, capture the era, while break-ins, fires, shootings, and the infamous blackout bring a harrowing sense of danger and intensity ... An important story of one of New York City's most dangerous times." —Kirkus Reviews (starred review)

"Powerfully moving, this stellar piece of historical fiction emphasizes the timeless concerns of family loyalty and personal strength, while highlighting important issues that still resonate today." —Booklist (starred review)

ABOUT THE AUTHOR: **Meg Medina** is the author of YA novels *Yaqui Delgado Wants to Kick Your Ass*, which received the Pura Belpré Author Award, and *The Girl Who Could Silence the Wind*, as well as the picture books *Mango, Abuela, and Me* and *Tía Isa Wants a Car*, winner of an Ezra Jack Keats New Writer Award. She lives in Richmond, Virginia.

March 2016 | Hardcover | Young Adult | 320 pp | $17.99 | ISBN 9780763674670
Candlewick Press | Candlewick.com | MegMedina.com

CONVERSATION STARTERS

1. "I tell a thousand little lies about my life every day so I can feel like a normal person," says Nora (205). What do you think is the biggest lie that Nora tells? Why does she tell it?

2. Feminism was on the rise in 1977. What opportunities did the movement offer young women like Nora and Kathleen? What did it mean to older women like Stiller and Mrs. MacInerney? Why were some women, like Mima, appalled by it?

3. "You think we suck as feminists?" Kathleen asks Nora at a women's rights rally (78). "We *do* argue about Wella Balsam versus Prell." What do you think is the difference between a good feminist and a bad one? Does worrying about hair care (or getting dressed up for boys) undermine Kathleen's and Nora's commitments to the cause?

4. Nora has a troubled relationship with both of her parents, but they aren't the only grown-ups in her life. Who are the other important adults? How do they support her? Why?

5. In what ways is 1977 very different from our own time? In what ways is it similar?

6. Why does Mimi demand more from her daughter than from her son? Would Hector be better off if she didn't? Would Nora?

7. "Sometimes it's easier to let people think I'm Greek or Italian," Nora says (115). Why does she sometimes feel the need to hide her ethnicity? What does being Latina mean to Nora and her mother?

8. "Remember to reach," Nora's guidance counselor tells her on the last day of school. "You'll surprise yourself" (215). What does Nora ultimately reach for? How is she surprised?

9. "Burn Baby Burn" is what Nora and Kathleen write on the beach at Breezy Point. What is the significance of that phrase to the two friends? What makes it such a fitting title for this book?

10. "I wrote this story," Meg Medina writes in her Author's Note, "because young people everywhere sometimes find that they have to fuel their hope against a bleak backdrop and outpourings of rage" (306). How does Nora fuel her hope? How have other young people in difficult situations, either in your community or elsewhere, fueled theirs?

THE EMPEROR OF ANY PLACE
Tim Wynne-Jones

When Evan's father dies suddenly, Evan finds a hand-bound yellow book on his desk—a book his dad had been reading when he passed away. The book is the diary of a Japanese soldier stranded on a small Pacific island in WWII. Why was his father reading it? What is in this account that Evan's grandfather, whom Evan has never met before, fears so much that he will do anything to prevent its being seen? And what could this possibly mean for Evan? In a pulse-quickening mystery evoking the elusiveness of truth and the endurance of wars passed from father to son, this engrossing novel is a suspenseful, at times terrifying read from award-winning author Tim Wynne-Jones.

"English-Canadian author Tim Wynne-Jones crafts a truly spellbinding novel in which the mystical, desert-island, wartime chronicle is as riveting as the modern-day story ... and the ways they begin to fuse together are breathtaking." —Shelf Awareness (starred review)

"An accomplished wordsmith, Wynne-Jones achieves an extraordinary feat: he eliminates the hidden depths of personalities and families through a mesmerizing blend of realism and magic." —Kirkus Reviews (starred review)

"A riveting, remarkable novel by a reliably great Canadian writer." —Booklist (starred review)

"Offering a unique take on the World War II period, this intergenerational tale is an excellent addition to most YA collections." —School Library Journal (starred review)

"An affecting and unforgettable read." —The Horn Book (starred review)

ABOUT THE AUTHOR: **Tim Wynne-Jones** is the accomplished author of numerous YA novels, including *Blink & Caution*, winner of the 2012 Boston Globe–Horn Book Award, and *The Uninvited*, short-listed for the Arthur Ellis Award and the Governor General's Literary Award. In 2012, Tim Wynne-Jones was named an Officer of the Order of Canada for his services to literature. He lives with his wife in Ontario.

October 2015 | Hardcover | Young Adult | 336 pp | $17.99 | ISBN 9780763669737
Candlewick Press | Candlewick.com | TimWynne-Jones.com

CONVERSATION STARTERS

1. Describe Evan as a character, including his life before his father died. How does he cope with his grief and anger?

2. Isamu comments on his father, who was harsh to him, and grandfather, who taught him about stories. Analyze his relationship with those two men and the effect it had on his sense of himself. Compare the relationships to those of Evan, Clifford, and Griff.

3. In the prologue to Isamu's book, Derwood calls it "a remarkable love story," referring to Isamu and Hisako (28). Discuss whether or not you agree. Find places where Isamu speaks to Hisako directly. What does it show about their relationship? How does writing to Hisako help Isamu?

4. When Isamu first encounters the ghost children, he thinks they will protect him from the other ghosts. Discuss who the ghost children are, what they do, and how they affect Isamu, Derwood, Griff, and Evan. How do they give Isamu hope? When Evan experiences being a ghost child on the island, what does he see?

5. Near the end of the book, Evan sees Griff as wearing a mask, which he also calls armor, that is slowly flaking off. Analyze the meaning of this metaphor and whether you find it effective. How does it tie in with the *bunraku* puppet show Isamu seems to see?

6. Isamu first sees *Tengu* when it attacks Derwood. He believes Derwood has brought it somehow. Describe *Tengu* and its role in the story for Isamu, Derwood, and Griff. Discuss it as a real creature and as a metaphor. Why does Isamu eventually think *Tengu* is his "master?"

7. Evan feels like he has washed up on a desert island "where he is surrounded by dead people ... and one person who should be dead" (110). Griff describes himself as having landed on a "hostile island" (143). Discuss the importance of islands in the novel.

8. Griff says about veterans, "Nobody really wants to know about them or the dirty business they're honor-bound to carry out" (288). Evan later sees a look on Griff's face that shows "a lifetime of people who didn't get him — didn't understand" (309). Discuss these quotes and what they say about Griff, his views on life, and his relationship to the world.

9. The book's epigraph is an excerpt from Dylan Thomas's poem "A Process in the Weather of the Heart." What is the emotional impact of these lines, and how does it set a tone for the novel?

THE HIRED GIRL
Laura Amy Schlitz

Fourteen-year-old Joan Skraggs, just like the heroines in her beloved novels, yearns for real life and true love. But what hope is there for adventure, beauty, or art on a hardscrabble farm in Pennsylvania where the work never ends? Over the summer of 1911, Joan pours her heart out into her diary as she seeks a new, better life for herself—because maybe, just maybe, a hired girl cleaning and cooking for six dollars a week can become what a farm girl could only dream of—a woman with a future. Newbery Medalist Laura Amy Schlitz relates Joan's journey from the muck of the chicken coop to the comforts of a society household in Baltimore taking readers on an exploration of feminism and housework; religion and literature; love and loyalty; cats, hats, and bunions.

"The beauty of this novel is that it dares to go beyond the school-is-cruel and paranormal-dystopian-romance conventions and lets its adolescent heroine think on the page about what makes a human being whole: art, love, faith, education, family, friendship." —The New York Times Book Review

"Fans of Little Women, *rejoice. Janet's impassioned diary, inspired by Schlitz's own grandmother's journals, explores themes of faith and feminism, love and literature, culture and class in early 20th-century America, all the while charming readers with a vivid cast of characters." —Shelf Awareness*

"A memorable novel from a captivating storyteller." —Booklist (starred review)

"A highly satisfying and smart breast-clutcher." —Kirkus Reviews (starred review)

"Coming-of-age drama and deeper questions of faith, belonging, and womanhood are balanced with just the right blend of humor. A wonderful look into the life of a strong girl who learns that she needs the love of others to truly grow up." —School Library Journal (starred review)

ABOUT THE AUTHOR: **Laura Amy Schlitz** is the author of the Newbery Medal–winning *Good Masters! Sweet Ladies! Voices from a Medieval Village,* the Newbery Honor Book and *The New York Times* bestseller *Splendors and Glooms.* A teacher as well as a writer, Laura Amy Schlitz lives in Maryland.

March 2015 | Paperback | Young Adult | 192 pp | $12.99 | ISBN 9780763673680
Candlewick Press | Candlewick.com

CONVERSATION STARTERS

1. "I know I'm not nothing," Joan writes while she's still living on the farm (36). What is the source of her self-confidence? How did her mother and teacher foster it? Why can't her father and brothers extinguish it?

2. Why does Mr. Skraggs burn his daughter's books? What does he fear reading will do to her? Is he right? Why or why not?

3. "She is utterly without guile," Mrs. Rosenbach says of Joan, "a stranger in a strange land" (94). What does Mrs. Rosenbach mean? Have you ever felt like a stranger in a strange land? Do you think Mrs. Rosenbach ever felt like one?

4. Joan had never met a Jew or heard the word "anti-Semitism" before she went to Baltimore. What does living with the Rosenbachs teach her about the city's Jewish population? What does she discover about anti-Semitism in Baltimore and beyond?

5. Social class separates Joan from the Rosenbachs perhaps even more than religion. How are hired girls supposed to behave? What are the penalties for breaking the rules?

6. Discuss Mr. Rosenbach's relationship with Joan. How is it different from his wife's relationship with the hired girl?

7. What does Mimi realize immediately about Joan? Why does she think of Joan as a friend, not as a servant? What traits do the two girls share?

8. "You think of yourself as a member of this family," Mimi says to Joan "as if you're almost Jewish. But you're not. You'll never be one of us" (327). Why is this so hurtful for Joan to hear? Why could she never be David's wife?

9. At the very beginning of the book, when Joan receives her new diary, she vows to "write in it with *truth* and *refinement*" (3). By the end of *The Hired Girl*, has she kept that promise? Why or why not?

10. Joan begins the novel lamenting the lost opportunity to get an education, and she ends it rejoicing because she's about to go to school. In between, she falls in love with David Rosenbach. As a reader, were you disappointed that Joan's first love affair ended in heartbreak (and recovery)? Would you have rather had the book end with her engagement to David? Why or why not?

HOLLOW CITY
Ransom Riggs

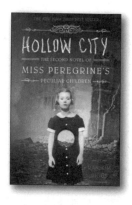

The extraordinary journey that began in *Miss Peregrine's Home for Peculiar Children* continues as Jacob Portman and his newfound friends journey to London, the peculiar capital of the world. There, they hope to find a cure for their beloved headmistress, Miss Peregrine. But in this war-torn city, hideous surprises lurk around every corner. And before Jacob can deliver the peculiar children to safety, he must make an important decision about his love for Emma Bloom.

Hollow City draws readers in a richly imagined world of telepathy and time loops, of sideshows and shapeshifters—a world populated with adult "peculiars," murderous wights, and a bizarre menagerie of uncanny animals. Like its predecessor, this second novel in the Peculiar Children series blends thrilling fantasy with never-before-published vintage photography for a one-of-a-kind reading experience.

" ... *a stunning achievement.*" —*The Boston Globe*

"*I was blown away ...* Hollow City *is fantastic ...* " —USAToday.com

"*New readers of the series will find this novel a treat ... Fans of the first title will find this book a treasure.*" —*School Library Journal*

ABOUT THE AUTHOR: **Ransom Riggs** grew up in Florida but now makes his home in the land of peculiar children—Los Angeles. He was raised on a steady diet of ghost stories and British comedy, which probably explains the novels he writes. There's a nonzero chance he's in your house right now, watching you from underneath the bed. (Go ahead and check. We'll wait.) If not, you can always find him on Twitter @ransomriggs.com.

February 2015 | Paperback | Young Adult | 416 pp | $10.99 | ISBN 9781594747359
Quirk Books | QuirkBooks.com | RansomRiggs.com

CONVERSATION STARTERS

1. At the end of *Miss Peregrine's Home for Peculiar Children*, the children are starting out on a new, hopeful adventure. Though *Hollow City* begins where the previous book left off, what has changed about the children's outlook? Do they still have hope?

2. Enoch tends to be the antagonist within the group. Do you think Enoch is pessimistic or realistic?

3. Why do you think the hollows and wights chose to pose as Nazi soldiers? How does this element add to their malicious presence in the book?

4. The children spend the entire book running away from hollows while trying to make their way to London. Did you think running was the best plan, or should they have tried to stand and fight, or simply hide?

5. Enoch repeatedly voices the worst-case scenario. Does doing so harm or hurt the group's progress? Is it better to keep spirits high by sugarcoating the truth or to be completely honest about the situation and prepare to face it?

6. The Gypsies live separately from the rest of society, much like the peculiar children. What other similarities do you notice between the Gypsies and the peculiars?

7. The children's stories of their past are mostly sad, especially Emma's. How would you react if your friend or family member suddenly developed peculiar powers?

8. What did you think about Jacob's eventual decision to leave the peculiar children? What decision would you have made in his place?

9. *Hollow City* ends with a spectacular cliffhanger. What do you think will happen in the next book? How will Jacob's newly discovered powers affect the story?

10. If the books in the Peculiar Children series were made into films, whom would you cast to play Jacob?

THE HUNDRED LIES OF LIZZIE LOVETT

Chelsea Sedoti

Hawthorn wasn't trying to insert herself into a missing person's investigation. Or maybe she was. But that's only because Lizzie Lovett's disappearance is the one fascinating mystery their sleepy town has ever had. Bad things don't happen to popular girls like Lizzie Lovett, and Hawthorn is convinced she'll turn up at any moment—which means the time for speculation is now.

So Hawthorn comes up with her own theory for Lizzie's disappearance. A theory way too absurd to take seriously...at first. The more Hawthorn talks, the more she believes. And what better way to collect evidence than to immerse herself in Lizzie's life? Like getting a job at the diner where Lizzie worked and hanging out with Lizzie's boyfriend. After all, it's not as if he killed her—or did he?

Told with a unique voice that is both hilarious and heart-wrenching, Hawthorn's quest for proof may uncover the greatest truth is within herself.

"This novel is full of topics that are relevant to teens, bullying, self-esteem, family dynamics and suicide. Well Done!" —**Holly Frakes, Schuler Books and Music (Okemos, MI)**

ABOUT THE AUTHOR: **Chelsea Sedoti** lives in Las Vegas, Nevada. Her short stories have been published in *Pantheon Magazine* and *Balloons Lit Journal*. She went to school for film and worked as a videographer before switching to writing. Chelsea spends her time rock climbing, baking, and exploring the Mojave Desert.

January 2017 | Hardcover | Young Adult | 400 pp | $17.99 | ISBN 9781492636083
Sourcebooks Fire | Sourcebooks.com | ChelseaSedoti.com

CONVERSATION STARTERS

1. When Lizzie Lovett first disappears, the town is upset, but Hawthorn is ambivalent. As time passes, their roles reverse. Is there a reason for this shift? If it were you, how might you have reacted?

2. As Hawthorn discovers, sometimes expectations can ruin an experience. What expectations did Hawthorn have that turned out vastly different from what she imagined? What was her reaction to these situations?

3. Is Hawthorn's relationship with Enzo positive or negative? By the end of the book, has it helped her grow or harmed her?

4. What gives people like Mychelle so much power? Is the bullying Hawthorn faces a product of her own actions? Is there something she could or should have done to prevent it?

5. Do you agree with Emily's decision to take a break from Hawthorn? Was she being a good or bad friend by doing so?

6. We all wear masks and try to let people see only what we want them to. During the story, whose masks are removed and what is revealed? What does Hawthorn learn about the difference between knowing someone and knowing about someone?

7. Discuss Enzo's painting of Hawthorn. What's the difference between seeing Hawthorn for who she is versus creating a painting of how she sees the world? How is one better than the other?

8. Does Hawthorn genuinely believe in her farfetched theory about Lizzie's disappearance? If so, what does this say about her? If not, why do you think she aggressively pursues the theory? What does this fantasy offer to Hawthorn?

9. Hawthorn is profoundly impacted when the truth about Lizzie's disappearance is discovered. Why do you think she reacted the way she did?

10. Hawthorn creates fictions about many people. Why do you think she does this? If you were a student in school with Hawthorn, what fictions might she create about your life?

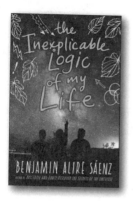

THE INEXPLICABLE LOGIC OF MY LIFE

Benjamin Alire Sáenz

From multi-award winning author and poet Benjamin Alire Sáenz, author of *Aristotle and Dante Discover the Secrets of the Universe*, comes a story of family and friendship, life and death, and one teen struggling to understand who he is.

The first day of senior year: Everything is about to change. Until this moment, Sal has always been certain of his place with his adoptive gay father and their loving Mexican-American family.

But now his own history unexpectedly haunts him, and life-altering events force him and his best friend, Samantha, to confront issues of faith, loss, and grief. Sal discovers that he no longer knows who he really is—but if Sal's not who he thought he was, who is he?

"Friendships, family, grief, joy, rage, faith, doubt, poetry, and love—this complex and sensitive book has room for every aspect of growing up!" —**Margarita Engle, Newbery Honor-Winning** author of The Surrender Tree

"A needed, lovely, and powerful book." —**Connie Griffin, Bookworks (Albuquerque, NM)**

"What the world needs now is a book like this one. A book filled with warmth and wisdom, about the families we create. Profoundly important and moving. Read it." —**Bill Konigsberg,** award-winning author of *Openly Straight* and *The Porcupine of Truth*

"Thought-provoking and uplifting, this is a compelling coming-of-age novel in which well-drawn, witty, independent, resilient, and reflective characters search for life meaning and their true selves. It treats the vicissitudes of life with wonder, and the complexities of being human with compassion, and—above all—love." —**Francisco Jiménez, Pura Belpré Honor-winning** author of *Breaking Through* and *Reaching Out*

ABOUT THE AUTHOR: **Benjamin Alire Sáenz** is an acclaimed writer for adults and teens. His novel *Aristotle and Dante Discover the Secrets of the Universe* won a Printz Honor Award, the Pura Belpre, Lambda, and Stonewall Book Awards. Mr. Sáenz lives in El Paso. TX.

March 2017 | Hardcover | Young Adult | 464 pp | $17.99 | ISBN 9780544586505
Clarion Books | hmhco.com

CONVERSATION STARTERS

1. In the course of the novel, Sal, a senior in high school, questions his identity and his place in the world. These are issues many teenagers face at this stage of life. What is it about this transitional period that invites so much self-reflection?

2. Sal has a strong relationship with his adopted father, Vicente, who imparts to him a sensitivity that Sal fears is at odds with his genetic makeup and a deep-rooted sense of anger he can't shake. What are your thoughts about "nature versus nurture" in this context, and how do you think Sal's adoption has affected his development?

3. Talk about Sal's struggle to come to terms with his racial identity as a Caucasian boy living with an adopted family that is Mexican-American. How does the fact of his ethnic background affect his feelings toward his family and his feelings of inclusivity, and how does that evolve as the novel progresses?

4. Sal's relationship with his best friend, Samantha, is unusual in YA literature, as they have a solid friendship with no romantic complications. What do you think has drawn these characters together, and what makes their relationship so solid?

5. Vicente faces prejudice in this novel, tied to both his sexuality and to his ethnicity. Talk about his reactions to these encounters (such as his conversation with Mr. Infante) and what his responses say about his character.

6. Sal's relationship with Mima is particularly special. How do you think Mima's words of wisdom to Sal shape his actions and his relationships with the other characters?

7. Sam's relationship with her mother is one of the more contentious pairings in the novel. Talk about Sam's complex feelings toward her mother, and how those feelings evolve as the novel unfolds.

8. When Vicente's former boyfriend Marcos comes back into the picture, what is Sal's reaction? Why does Sal struggle to accept Marcos, and what does Vicente's approach to the situation say about his relationship with his son?

9. Sal's friend Fito has his share of struggles in the novel, including being kicked out of his own house by his mother. Talk about each of the characters' responses to Fito's plight (Sal, Sam, Vicente, Marcos) and what it says about each of them.

INTO WHITE
Randi Pink

LaToya Williams lives in Birmingham, Alabama, and attends a mostly white high school. She's so low on the social ladder that even the other black kids disrespect her. Only her older brother, Alex, believes in her. At least, until a higher power answers her only prayer--to be "anything but black." And voila! She wakes up with blond hair, blue eyes, and lily white skin. And then the real fun begins . . .

ABOUT THE AUTHOR: **Randi Pink** grew up in the South and attended a mostly white high school. She lives in Birmingham, Alabama, with her husband, and works for a local public radio station. *Into White* is her fiction debut.

September 2016 | Hardcover | Young Adult | 288 pp | $17.99 | ISBN 9781250070210
Feiwel & Friends | MacKids.com | RandiPink.com

CONVERSATION STARTERS

1. At the beginning of the book, Toya's interaction with another student fuels her wish to change. What is it about this interaction with Deante that pushes Toya to a breaking point? What do you imagine her life in high school has been like up to this time?

2. Toya appears white to everyone except her parents and her brother. Why do you think the author decided this?

3. After her transformation Toya and Alex visit an upscale department store where a salesperson questions why they are hanging out together. How realistic do you believe this is? Has anything like this ever happened to you or a friend?

4. Toya's parents believe that by living in a mostly white neighborhood and sending Toya and Alex to a mostly white high school, they are giving their kids better opportunities than they had. Do you agree with their decisions? Why or why not? What aspects of Toya's relationship with her parents mirror your own dynamic with one or both of your parents?

5. The girls who accept Toya once she becomes "Kat" are popular and socially influential at school. Why wouldn't these girls have befriended Toya before her transformation? Is it only about appearance for these girls?

6. Alex is keeping a secret from Toya about his future. Why doesn't he confide in her?

7. Toya has had a crush on Josh for a long time before her transformation. Why did she like him and how do her feelings change as she gets to know him?

8. There is one more person who sees through "Kat" and recognizes Toya: Deante. Why do you believe the author made this choice? Why has Deante kept some things hidden from Toya and the rest of the school?

9. Describe Toya's feelings after Deante takes her to the sorority event on campus. Why is this event so key in the story?

10. What do you see happening in Toya's life after the book ends? Will she change? Will her family dynamic change? What do you predict she will do after high school?

11. Does *Into White* help start conversations about race? Why or why not?

THE LIE TREE
Frances Hardinge

Read this thought-provoking, critically acclaimed novel (6 starred reviews!) from Frances Hardinge, winner of the Costa Book of the Year, Costa Children's Book Award, and Horn Book-Boston Globe Award.

Faith Sunderly leads a double life. To most people, she is reliable, dull, trustworthy—a proper young lady who knows her place as inferior to men. But inside, Faith is full of questions and curiosity, and she cannot resist mysteries: an unattended envelope, an unlocked door. She knows secrets no one suspects her of knowing. She knows that her family moved to the close-knit island of Vane because her famous scientist father was fleeing a reputation-destroying scandal. And she knows, when her father is discovered dead shortly thereafter, that he was murdered. In pursuit of justice and revenge, Faith hunts through her father's possessions and discovers a strange tree. The tree bears fruit only when she whispers a lie to it. The fruit of the tree, when eaten, delivers a hidden truth. The tree might hold the key to her father's murder—or it may lure the murderer directly to Faith herself.

"Readers of historical fiction, mystery, and fantasy will all be captivated by this wonderfully crafted novel and the many secrets hidden within its pages." —*Booklist* (starred review)

"Some of the most beloved science-fiction and fantasy writers, from Madeleine L'Engle to Philip Pullman, began as young-adult authors whose fiction proved so compelling that adult readers embraced it as well, ignoring the line that supposedly separates these audiences. One of the latest such writers is Frances Hardinge." —*Chicago Tribune*

ABOUT THE AUTHOR: **Frances Hardinge** is the winner of the Costa Book of the Year and Costa Children's Book Awards for *The Lie Tree*. She is the author of several books for children, including *Cuckoo Song* (five starred reviews, shortlisted for the Carnegie Medal), *The Lost Conspiracy* (five starred reviews, *Los Angeles Times* Book Award Finalist), *Fly by Night* (shortlisted for the Guardian Children's Book prize), *Well Witched* (SLJ Best Book of 2008), and *Fly Trap* (shortlisted for the Guardian Prize, longlisted for the Carnegie Medal). She lives in England.

April 2017 | Hardcover | Young Adult | 377 pp | $17.95 | ISBN 9781419718953
Amulet Books | AbramsBooks.com | FrancesHardinge.com

CONVERSATION STARTERS

1. Faith idolizes her father, the Reverend Erasmus Sunderly, a brilliant, forbidding man whose scientific work has brought him renown and, as we soon learn, disgrace. What information does she find out about him through the course of the book, and how does this affect her perception of him?

2. In sharp contrast, Faith considers her mother, Myrtle, shallow and scheming. What is Mrs. Sunderly's role in the household? How does she explain her actions to her daughter? What do the two learn from each other?

3. The Sunderly family has relocated from Kent to Vane, an isolated island where a scientific excavation is taking place. What sparked their move—overtly and covertly? What elements does the location add to the suspense and mystery of the narrative? How do you think things would have turned out had the Sunderlys stayed in Kent?

4. Reverend Sunderly is both a minister and a natural scientist. How does he attempt to reconcile his religious beliefs with the theory of evolution, as laid out in Charles Darwin's *On the Origin of Species*? What does Faith believe?

5. Although *The Lie Tree* initially appears to be an historical suspense novel, it is the Lie Tree itself—a fantastical, almost mythological invention—that steers it into other territory. What does the Lie Tree represent to each of the characters who knows about it? How does it change those who tend it? What does it do to Faith?

6. By the end of the book, Faith has fought for and achieved acknowledgment of her intellect, as well as her innate bravery; in other words, she is a feminist. What other strong women appear in this book, and how does their strength manifest? What sacrifices have they made to achieve their goals?

7. Which aspects of the book has Frances Hardinge drawn from actual historical record, and which are her own invention? What are the many different genres that she has blended into *The Lie Tree*?

8. Every major character in the novel has at least one secret – either an important piece of information, or something about themselves that they prefer to conceal. What are those secrets, how do they benefit the characters, and how are they revealed (if, in fact, they are)?

MY BEST FRIEND'S EXORCISM
Grady Hendrix

Abby and Gretchen have been best friends since fourth grade. Through the years, they have bonded over *E.T.*, roller-skating, and a shared love for pop music. But when they arrive at high school, things change. Gretchen begins to act ... different. As the strange coincidences and bizarre behavior start to pile up, Abby realizes there's only one possible explanation: Gretchen, her favorite person in the world, has a demon living inside her. And Abby is not about to let anyone or anything come between her and her best friend. With help from some unlikely allies, Abby embarks on a quest to save Gretchen. But is their friendship powerful enough to beat the devil?

"If The Exorcist *had been authored by Tina Fey instead of William Peter Blatty, it might have borne an uncanny resemblance to what Grady Hendrix has accomplished with* My Best Friend's Exorcism... *Fans of satire, nostalgia, dark comedy and, well, demons should read this book." —BookPage*

"Readers who thought Heathers *wasn't quite bleak enough will find this darkly humorous horror tale—filled with spot-on '80s pop-culture references—totally awesome." —Booklist* **(starred review)**

*"Sharply written ... Hendrix has made strong progress as a novelist, and this book makes a convincing case for his powers as a sharp observer of human behavior, filtered through a fun genre conceit that doesn't skimp on the spooky—or the bodily fluids." —***The A.V. Club**

ABOUT THE AUTHOR: **Grady Hendrix's** first novel, *Horrorstör*, an illustrated novel about a haunted big-box furniture store, was named one of the best books of 2014 by NPR. *Horrorstör* was translated into more than 10 languages; television rights were optioned to producer Gail Berman of Fox Networks Group. Hendrix has also written for various magazines. He lives in New York City, where he and his wife own and operate the acclaimed vegetarian restaurant Dirt Candy.

May 2016 | Hardcover | Fiction | 336 pp | $19.99 | ISBN 9781594748622
Quirk Books | QuirkBooks.com | GradyHendrix.com

CONVERSATION STARTERS

1. Hendrix took inspiration from his high school experience to inform *My Best Friend's Exorcism*. Were there any aspects of the book that you recognize from your own high school experience?

2. The book takes place during the Cold War and era of "satanic panic" when there was a sense that the United States was vulnerable to just about any type of evil. How do you think this historical backdrop affects the behavior of the characters?

3. Music is at the center of Abby and Gretchen's friendship. What '80s song do you relate most with?

4. *E.T. the Extra-Terrestrial* is a large part of Abby's life. In what other ways does '80s pop culture inform Abby and Gretchen's friendship?

5. We're introduced to the friendship between the four girls—Abby, Gretchen, Margaret, and Glee—fairly early on in the novel. What were your first impressions of the clique?

6. The girls' decision to drop acid is a turning point in the novel. How do you think this rite of passage affects the girls' relationships?

7. Abby and Gretchen come from different sides of the tracks. How do you think this affects their relationship as they grow up?

8. Gretchen, while under the influence of the devil, does a lot of terrible things. Which do you think is the worst?

9. Abby is a devoted friend. How far would you go if your best friend was possessed by the devil?

PERFECT LIARS
Kimberly Reid

Andrea Faraday is junior class valedictorian at the exclusive Woodruff School, where she was voted Most Likely to Do Everything Right. But looks can be deceiving. When her parents disappear, her life—and her Perfect Girl charade—begins to crumble, and her scheme to put things right just takes the situation from bad to so much worse. Pretty soon she's struck up the world's least likely friendship with the juvenile delinquents at Justice Academy, the last exit on the road to jail—and the first stop on the way out.

If she were telling it straight, friendship might not be the right word to describe their alliance, since Drea and her new associates could not be more different. She's rich and privileged; they're broke and, well, criminal. But Drea's got a secret: she has more in common with the juvie kids than they'd ever suspect. When it turns out they share a common enemy, Drea suggests they join forces to set things right. Sometimes, to save the day, a good girl's gotta be bad.

"The characters establish an effective, if hasty, alliance that readers can't help but root for as the author demonstrates her continued command of the mystery plot. Gripping, suspenseful, and refreshingly diverse." —Kirkus Reviews (**starred review**)

"Reid grounds her story in reality, with a diverse cast (Drea is biracial, Xavier is Korean-American), moral gray areas (involving juvenile offenders, attorneys, cops, and more), and ample consideration of the real-life consequences of the characters' actions." —Publishers Weekly

"An incredibly smart, compellingly original story with layered characters whose sparks fly off the page ... Kimberly Reid is an astonishing talent and Perfect Liars *is a perfect escape!"* —**Sarah Skilton, author of** *Bruised* **and** *High and Dry*

ABOUT THE AUTHOR: **Kimberly Reid** is the author of the Langdon Prep young adult mystery series starting with *My Own Worst Frenemy*, and the Colorado Book Award-winning memoir *No Place Safe*. She currently lives near Denver, Colorado, but her roots are firmly planted in Georgia clay and she still calls Atlanta home.

May 2016 | Hardcover | Young Adult | 384 pp | $19.95 | ISBN 9781620142738
Tu Books/Lee & Low Books | LeeandLow.com | KimberlyReid.com

CONVERSATION STARTERS

1. In the beginning of the story, Drea has a strong independent streak, almost to the point of being aloof. Why does Drea struggle to make friends and to trust others? Why does her outlook change around friendship and camaraderie?

2. How does Drea's perception of adolescents in the juvenile justice system change?

3. Why is Drea ashamed of how her family attained its privilege?

4. What connection can be made between Damon's choices (becoming a police officer) and Drea's choices (in unrelenting pursuit of perfectionism) and the choices of their parents (being con artists)?

5. Drea's friends at the Justice Academy solve the problem with the very skills that led them to being in the juvenile justice system. What do you think the author, Kimberly Reid, wants readers to take away?

6. Look up imposter syndrome and "Duck Syndrome." Do either of these describe Drea's experiences? Is her pursuit of perfectionism unique to Drea's personality and internal pressures or are there systemic pressures as well? How might Drea's gender contribute to her anxiety and stress in being perfect? Does Drea face additional pressures or unfair expectations to be successful because she is biracial in an elite, mostly white prep school?

7. How are Drea and Xavier similar?

8. Do Drea and Xavier see each other as equals? Why or why not?

9. Examine the reasons that led to Gigi, Xavier, and Jason each being in the juvenile justice system. Do their actions define them as "bad" people? Does their involvement with Drea mean they are redeemed?

10. Which characters do you particularly admire or dislike?

11. Unlike the students Drea meets at Justice Academy, she has had access to elite institutions, privileged experiences, and influential people. Does Drea make the most of these resources?

12. Drea strives to be independent and self-sufficient. Does she achieve the freedom she seeks? Why or why not?

13. What impact do you think Drea's experience in collaborating with the students at the Justice Academy might have on her view of her parents' choices and lifestyle?

RAIN REIGN
Ann M. Martin

A *New York Times* Bestseller

Rose Howard is obsessed with homonyms. She's thrilled that her own name is a homonym, and she purposely gave her dog Rain a name with two homonyms (Reign, Rein), which, according to Rose's rules of homonyms, is very special. Not everyone understands Rose's obsessions, her rules, and the other things that make her different—not her teachers, not other kids, and not her single father. When a storm hits their rural town, rivers overflow, the roads are flooded, and Rain goes missing. Rose's father shouldn't have let Rain out. Now Rose has to find her dog, even if it means leaving her routines and safe places to search.

"Rose is a character we root for every step of the way. She is resilient, honest, and, in her own odd way, very perceptive; a most reliable narrator." **—*The Horn Book*** (starred review)

"Readers will empathize with Rose, who finds strength and empowerment through her unique way of looking at the world." **—*School Library Journal*** (starred review)

"Simplicity, clarity, and emotional resonance are hallmarks of Rose's first-person narrative ... A strong story told in a nuanced, highly accessible way." **—*Kirkus Reviews,*** (starred review)

"Martin has penned a riveting, seamless narrative in which each word sings and each scene counts." **—*Booklist*** (starred review)

*"Newbery Honor author Martin (*A Corner of the Universe*) is extremely successful in capturing Rose's perspective and personality . . ."* **—*Publishers Weekly*** (starred review)

ABOUT THE AUTHOR: **Ann M. Martin** is the author of *Ten Rules for Living with My Sister, Ten Good and Bad Things About My Life*, and *Everything for a Dog*, all from Feiwel and Friends. She won a Newbery Honor Award for *A Corner of the Universe*, and is the author of the beloved Baby-sitters Club series. She lives in upstate New York.

October 2014 | Hardcover | Young Adult | 256 pp | $16.99 | ISBN 9780312643003
Feiwel & Friends | MacKids.com | RainReign.com

CONVERSATION STARTERS

1. Rose Howard narrates her own story. Discuss the difference between a "reliable" narrator and an "unreliable" one. Which is Rose? Why?

2. Rose's list of homonyms is one of her most important possessions. Why do you think she keeps this list? There are probably easier ways to update it (on a computer, for instance). Why is Rose's list handwritten?

3. Everyone is different; every person has particular habits and interests. And some people have differences that others see as "disabilities." What makes Rose different? Are her outbursts in class something she does on purpose?

4. How does Rain help Rose? Describe the roles that pets play in the lives of people who love them.

5. Do you believe Rose's father let Rain out of the house with any bad intentions? Why or why not?

6. Why is Rose's uncle Weldon more patient with Rose than her own father?

7. Do you agree with Rose's decisions about Rain? Describe what might have happened if Rose had acted differently.

8. Discuss Rose's future—what lies ahead for her once the book is finished?

SURVIVOR'S CLUB: THE TRUE STORY OF A VERY YOUNG PRISONER OF AUSCHWITZ

Michael Bornstein
and Debbie Bornstein Holinstat

In 1945, in a now-famous piece of archival footage, four-year-old Michael Bornstein was filmed by Soviet soldiers as he was carried out of Auschwitz in his grandmother's arms. Here is the unforgettable story of how a father's courageous wit, a mother's fierce love, and one perfectly timed illness saved his life, and how others in his family from Zarki, Poland, dodged death time and again with incredible deftness. Working from his own recollections as well as extensive interviews with other family members and survivors who knew the family, Michael relates his inspirational story with the help of his daughter, Debbie Bornstein Holinstat. Shocking, heartbreaking, and ultimately uplifting, this narrative nonfiction offers an indelible depiction of what happened to one Polish village in the wake of the German invasion in 1939.

ABOUT THE AUTHORS: **Michael Bornstein** survived for seven months inside Auschwitz, where the average lifespan of a child was just two weeks. After the war, Michael reunited with his mother, who had been deported to an Austrian labor camp. Together, they immigrated to New York City in 1951. Michael earned his Ph.D. and worked in pharmaceutical research and development for more than forty years. Now retired, Michael lives with his wife in New York City and and speaks frequently to schools and other groups about his experiences in the Holocaust.

Debbie Bornstein Holinstat is Michael's third of four children. A producer for NBC and MSNBC News, she lives in North Caldwell, New Jersey. She also visits schools with her father, and has been working with him for two years, helping him research and write this memoir, although she has grown up hearing many of these stories her entire life.

March 2017 | Hardcover | Young Adult | 256 pp | $16.99 | ISBN 9780374305710
Farrar, Straus and Giroux (BYR) | SurvivorsClubBook.com | MBornstein.com

CONVERSATION STARTERS

1. We saw in the book that choices were sometimes the difference between life and death, horror and escape, for Michael and his family. Other times, it was luck and good timing that made the difference. In Michael's particular case, which do you think was more significant in accounting for his survival?

2. In the book, Ruth's parents gave her away twice to neighbors who promised to take care of her, but she ended up at an orphanage. Evaluate the decisions the housekeeper and the shoemaker made: do you agree with their choices?

3. If you lived in Poland during the Holocaust, what might you have done? Do you think you would have made the choices that Michael's parents made—such as staying in the open ghetto until the end—or would you have searched for a family willing to hide you in an attic like Ruth's family did?

4. If you were a non-Jewish person living in Poland, do you think you would have risked your life and your family's safety to harbor a Jew in your attic?

5. Why do you think Hitler rose to power and got away with ordering his Nazi military to commit such horrible crimes against Jews and other minority groups?

6. Today there is still evidence of anti-Semitism all over the world. Why do you think there are people who dislike Jews? Are there other minority groups who face similar persecution today?

7. Despite well-documented evidence of the Nazi crimes, there are some who still deny that the Holocaust happened. Why is it difficult for some people to confront and accept negative events in history? How can we respond to Holocaust deniers?

8. Jewish people often use the motto "Never forget" when talking about the Holocaust. Once the last of the survivors is gone, will future generations forget what happened to Jews and other persecuted minorities during World War II? What can each of us do to make sure future generations "Never forget"?

9. How do the crimes against humanity committed by Hitler and the Nazis demonstrate the need for a "zero tolerance" policy against bullying in our everyday lives?

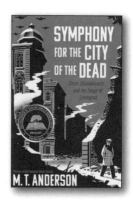

SYMPHONY FOR THE CITY OF THE DEAD: DMITRI SHOSTAKOVICH AND THE SIEGE OF LENINGRAD

M. T. Anderson

In September 1941, Adolf Hitler's Wehrmacht surrounded Leningrad in what was to become one of the longest and most destructive sieges in Western history—almost three years of bombardment and starvation that culminated in the harsh winter of 1943–1944. More than a million citizens perished. Survivors recall corpses littering the frozen streets, their relatives having neither the means nor the strength to bury them. Residents burned books, furniture, and floorboards to keep warm; they ate family pets and—eventually—one another to stay alive. Trapped between the Nazi invading force and the Soviet government itself was composer Dmitri Shostakovich, who would write a symphony that roused, rallied, eulogized, and commemorated his fellow citizens—the Leningrad Symphony, which came to occupy a surprising place of prominence in the eventual Allied victory. This is the true story of a city under siege: the triumph of bravery and defiance in the face of terrifying odds. It is also a look at the power—and layered meaning—of music in beleaguered lives.

"It's the work of an author who has never jumped onto any trend-wagon, but has instead followed his own keen intelligence toward a big, essential story."
—**New York Journal of Books**

"A triumphant story of bravery and defiance that will shock and inspire."
—**Kirkus Reviews** (starred review)

"This ambitious and gripping work is narrative nonfiction at its best ... The book has all the intrigue of a spy thriller. This is also the story of survival against almost impossible odds. Through it all, Anderson weaves the thread of the composer's music and the role it played in this larger-than-life drama."
—**School Library Journal** (starred review)

ABOUT THE AUTHOR: **M. T. Anderson** is the author of *Feed*, winner of the *Los Angeles Times* Book Prize, as well as *The Astonishing Life of Octavian Nothing*, winner of the National Book Award and its sequel, *The Kingdom on the Waves*. Both volumes were *New York Times* bestsellers and Michael L. Printz Honor Books. M. T. Anderson lives in Cambridge, Massachusetts.

March 2015 | Paperback | Young Adult | 192 pp | $12.99 | ISBN 9780763673680
Candlewick Press | Candlewick.com | MT-Anderson.com

CONVERSATION STARTERS

1. Why does the author choose to open with the story of the microfilm? What other topics does he touch on in the prologue that prove important in the book? What storytelling elements does M. T. Anderson use to pull readers in and entice them to read the story?

2. Shostakovich was public admired at times and public derided at others. What caused the different opinions? What effect did this have on his life and family?

3. Violence and deprivation permeated the Soviet Union during this period. What were the goals of those perpetrating violence? How did the violence and deprivation affect cities and the country's cultural heritage? How did they affect families and daily life?

4. One of Shostakovich's friends said, "He learned to put on a mask he would wear for the rest of his life" (139). M. T. Anderson echoes this point in the author's note, describing the composer as "a man who learned to live behind a mask" (382). Note other examples of this metaphor as it relates to the composer's life, the lives of those around him, and the political situation.

5. "A symphony is built not just by the composer, the conductor, and the musicians, but by the audience" (281). This idea is raised more than once in the narrative. What does the author mean? How do audiences react differently to Shostakovich's symphonies in different places, including the United States.

6. Unlike many nonfiction authors, M. T. Anderson addresses the reader directly at times. In one example, he says, "It is easy for us all to imagine we are heroes when we are sitting in our kitchens, dreaming of distant suffering" (117). Discuss this approach and the reason the author takes it. What do you think of Anderson's overall point of view toward Shostakovich?

7. Anderson discusses problems with his sources and their reliability. He evaluates an anecdote about Shostakovich seeing Lenin (24-26). How does the author handle the uncertainty about its credibility? How does this relate to Anderson's comments on page 140 about the authenticity of Shotakovich's memoir and discussion in the author's note about the trustworthiness of sources in the Soviet era?

8. "Anderson writes in the prologue that "at its heart," the book is "a story about the power of music and its meanings" (7). Do you agree? Did music help people feel less alone?

THIS IS WHERE IT ENDS

Marieke Nijkamp

The New York Times **Bestseller**

Goodreads YA Best Book of the Month

BuzzFeed YA Book You Should Be Reading

Bustle 2016 Most Anticipated YA Novel

Book Riot 2016 Book You Should Mark Down Now

10:00 a.m.: The principal of Opportunity High School in Alabama finishes her speech, welcoming the entire student body to a new semester and encouraging them to excel and achieve.

10:02 a.m.: The students get up to leave the auditorium for their next class.

10:03 a.m.: The auditorium doors won't open.

10:05 a.m.: Someone starts shooting.

This explosive, emotional, page-turning debut about a high school held hostage for fifty-four harrowing minutes is told from the perspective of four teens—each with their own reason to fear the boy with the gun.

"This Is Where It Ends takes place over the course of just 54 heart-pounding minutes, but it tells a story that will stay with you much longer ... " —**Bustle**

"Gritty, emotional and suspenseful ... " —**BuzzFeed**

"Compelling." —**Book Riot**

"You'll finish this book in a single evening, guaranteed." —*Paste*

"Heart pounding and heart wrenching." —**Julie Murphy, author of** *Dumplin'*

"As long as there are Newtowns and Columbines there will be a desperate need for gripping, well-written, and poignant novels like this one." —**Todd Strasser, author of** *Give a Boy a Gun* **and** *Fallout*

ABOUT THE AUTHOR: **Marieke Nijkamp** is a storyteller, dreamer, globetrotter, geek. She holds degrees in philosophy, history, and medieval studies, and is a founding member of We Need Diverse Books, DiversifYA, and YA Misfits. She lives in the Netherlands.

January 2016 | Hardcover | Young Adult | 288 pp | $17.99 | ISBN 9781492622468
December 2016 | Paperback | Young Adult | 304 pp | $10.99 | ISBN 9781492622475
Sourcebooks Fire | Sourcebooks.com | MariekeNijkamp.com

CONVERSATION STARTERS

1. There are many different kinds of relationships in this novel: family, friendship, romantic. How do these relationships inform what is at stake for each of the main characters?

2. Each character reacts differently to the shooting. Choose two characters and describe how they responded. Do you agree with the decisions they made? How might you have acted differently?

3. *This Is Where It Ends* is interspersed with texts, social media posts, and blog excerpts. How do you think technology has affected the way we experience and respond to tragedy?

4. If you could save one character in this novel, who would you save and why?

5. Family is very important to Sylv, so much so that she's willing to give up her dream to take care of her mother. If you were in her shoes, would you do the same? Why or why not?

6. Sylv tries to save Steve and Asha because "we're all responsible for each other." What does Sylv mean by this? Do you agree?

7. Autumn and Sylv keep secrets from each other. Do you think this helps or hurts their relationship? Do you agree with their decisions or would you have encouraged them to speak up?

8. Autumn doesn't feel as if she belongs in Opportunity. She tells Sylv, "If I stay here, I don't think I'll matter." What does she mean by this?

9. While speaking of Autumn's mother, Autumn's father says, "Dance took everything from her." Is that the case for Autumn too? What did dance give her?

10. Early in the novel, Tomás has the opportunity to escape the school. Instead, he chooses to try to help his classmates. Discuss Tomás's decision. What would you have done?

11. When Fareed is on the phone with the police, Tomás comments that Fareed suppresses his accent so he won't be marked as a suspect. Do you think that was necessary? Do you think that is fair?

12. Claire and Chris feel helpless as they wait for news about what is happening inside the school. In your opinion, was it more difficult for the characters inside the auditorium or those waiting to hear about their loved ones? Why?

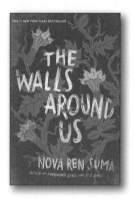

THE WALLS AROUND US
Nova Ren Suma

#1 *New York Times* Bestseller

An NPR Best Book of 2015

A *Boston Globe* Best Book of 2015

A *Book Riot* Best Book of 2015

2015 Edgar Award Nominee for Best Young Adult

The Walls Around Us is a ghostly story of suspense told in two voices—one still living and one dead. On the outside, there's Violet, an eighteen-year-old dancer days away from the life of her dreams when something threatens to expose the shocking truth of her achievement. On the inside, within the walls of a girls' juvenile detention center, there's Amber, locked up for so long she can't imagine freedom. Tying these two worlds together is Orianna, who holds the key to unlocking all the girls' darkest mysteries.

Nova Ren Suma tells a supernatural tale of guilt and innocence, and what happens when one is mistaken for the other.

"With evocative language, Suma subtly explores the balance of power between the talented and the mediocre, the rich and the poor, the brave and the cowardly ... To reveal more would be to uncover the bloody heart that beats beneath the floorboards of this urban-legend-tinged tale." **—The New York Times**

"A gorgeously written, spellbinding ghost story ... Nova Ren Suma's prose hums with such power and fury that when the explosions do happen, they seem unavoidable." —Chicago Tribune

"Unputdownable ... the well-paced plot reveals guilt, innocence, and dark truths that will not stay hidden." —The Boston Globe

"A suspenseful tour de force." **—Libba Bray, author of *The Diviners* and *A Great and Terrible Beauty***

ABOUT THE AUTHOR: **Nova Ren Suma** has an MFA in fiction from Columbia University and a BA in writing and photography from Antioch College and has been awarded a fiction fellowship from the New York Foundation for the Arts. She is the author of *Imaginary Girls* and *17 & Gone*.

March 2016 | Paperback | Young Adult | 336 pp | $9.95 | ISBN 9781616205904
Algonquin Young Readers | AlgonquinYoungReaders.com | NovaRen.com

CONVERSATION STARTERS

1. Is either Amber or Violet a sympathetic narrator? Why or why not?

2. On page 280, Amber says, "I couldn't know for sure if our newest inmate, Orianna Speerling, regretted going outside after her friend that day." What do you suspect?

3. When Orianna receives the only red cup in the dining hall, her reaction is markedly different than that of her fellow inmates. Why does she respond the way she does? Why do you think she influences the other girls' feelings about the red cup going forward? How does Ori change the mood of the inmates in general?

4. Three years after Ori's death, Violet still believes she is the inferior dancer, even though she's become the star. How do Violet's insecurity and jealousy shape her character and actions? Why does she remain jealous of Orianna even after Orianna's death?

5. Violet's account of the crime changes as she repeats her telling of it. What do you make of the different accounts she gives us over the course of the novel? Similarly, Amber gradually changes some details in the stories she tells us. How do the various versions of events—and their timing—affect your feelings about Violet and Amber? How do they affect your reading experience?

6. Why do you think being in charge of the book cart is so important to Amber?

7. On page 312, when the officers are counting the girls in the dining hall, Amber says, "It seems we are meant to stay at full capacity, which for this facility is forty-two girls." How does the number forty-two play a role in the novel? Why do you think the author decided it was important to keep the number of inmates at forty-two?

8. How did you interpret the ending? Do you think all readers will reach the same conclusion? Why or why not?

WHEN THE SEA TURNED TO SILVER
Grace Lin

A breathtaking, full-color illustrated fantasy inspired by Chinese folklore, a companion to the Newbery Honor winner *Where the Mountain Meets the Moon*.

Pinmei's gentle, loving grandmother always has the most exciting tales for her granddaughter and the other villagers. However, the peace is shattered one night when soldiers of the Emperor arrive and kidnap the storyteller.

Everyone knows that the Emperor wants something called the Luminous Stone That Lights the Night. Determined to have her grandmother returned, Pinmei embarks on a journey to find the Luminous Stone alongside her friend Yishan, a mysterious boy who seems to have his own secrets to hide. Together, the two must face obstacles usually found only in legends to find the Luminous Stone and save Pinmei's grandmother—before it's too late.

A fast-paced adventure that is extraordinarily written and beautifully illustrated, *When the Sea Turned to Silver* is a masterpiece companion novel to *Where the Mountain Meets the Moon* and *Starry River of the Sky*.

ABOUT THE AUTHOR: **Grace Lin** is the award-winning and bestselling author and illustrator of *Starry River of the Sky*, *Where the Mountain Meets the Moon*, *The Year of the Dog*, *The Year of the Rat*, *Dumpling Days*, and the Ling & Ting series, as well as picture books such as *The Ugly Vegetables* and *Dim Sum for Everyone!* Grace is a graduate of the Rhode Island School of Design and lives in Massachusetts.

October 2016 | Hardcover | Young Adult | 384 pp | $18.99 | ISBN 9780316125925
Little, Brown Books for Young Readers | lb-kids.com | GraceLinBlog.com

CONVERSATION STARTERS

1. Amah tells Pinmei, "I know that when it is time for you to do something, you will do it." Does Pinmei believe her?

2. After Amah tells the stonecutter, "Stories cannot tell all," he says, "I disagree. I think stories tell everything." Why does the stonecutter believe this and not the Storyteller?

3. Lady Meng says, "If one of the greatest joys is encountering a friend far from home, making a friend must be as well." How do friendships cause positive results throughout the book?

4. The stonecutter tells Amah, "Almost all men respect the Storyteller. You can make time disappear. You can bring us to places we have never dreamed of. You can make us feel sorrow and joy and peace. You have great magic." Amah says the stonecutter is flattering her. Why does she not see her own importance, and how is that similar to Pinmei's own struggle?

5. The Paper of Answers told the king and emperor that the secret to mortality is stories. What does this mean?

6. The Paper of Answers not only provides answers to questions, but can physically change people too. Why does it work differently with different people?

7. Joy to the Heart says, "Mortals are the only ones who can give immortality. . . I guess it's because it's the mortals who create the memories that last. Without those, immortals forget. They can even forget who they are, right?" Why do you think Yishan had forgotten who he was? What does this show about the importance of stories?

8. In *The Story of Our Mountain*, the new ruler is mocked by the Mountain Spirit who asks, "Do you know who you are? Will you ever know?" Why does this make the new ruler so angry?

9. Yishan tells Pinmei on page 360 that she is a friend he will never forget, and that is the only immortality that matters. On page 368, Pinmei says she finally understands. What does she understand?

10. The book ends with Pinmei beginning to tell a story. The story begins with "When the sea turned to silver," which is the same way the book begins, and is the title of the book. How is everything tied together? What story is now being told? Why is it fitting this last scene takes place in the Long Walkway?

WITH MALICE
Eileen Cook

For fans of *We Were Liars* and *The Girl on the Train* comes a chilling, addictive psychological thriller about a teenage girl who cannot remember the last six weeks of her life.

Eighteen-year-old Jill Charron's senior trip to Italy was supposed to be the adventure of a lifetime. And then the accident happened. Waking up in a hospital room, her leg in a cast, stitches in her face, and a big blank canvas where the last 6 weeks should be, Jill comes to discover she was involved in a fatal accident in her travels abroad. She was jetted home by her affluent father in order to receive quality care. Care that includes a lawyer. And a press team. Because maybe the accident ... wasn't an accident. Wondering not just what happened but what she did, Jill tries to piece together the events of the past six weeks before she loses her thin hold on her once-perfect life.

"Cinematic scene breaks and propulsive reveals will keep the pages furiously turning in this slow-burning but explosive thriller." —***Booklist*** (**starred review**)

"A creepy, satisfying thriller." —***Entertainment Weekly***

"The story is twisty, well-written, and so powerful that I felt as though I was reading about a true crime. Is there anything more complex or vicious than a teen girl? Especially one with secrets." —**Chevy Stevens, *The New York Times* bestselling author *Still Missing* and *Those Girls***

"Some books you read and forget immediately. Some you finish and want to start again immediately. This is one of the latter. Staggeringly smart, just enough sexy, and virtually seamless." —**Terra Elan McVoy, author of Edgar Finalist, *Criminal***

ABOUT THE AUTHOR: **Eileen Cook** is a multi-published author with her novels appearing in eight different languages. Her books have been optioned for film and TV. Eileen lives in Vancouver with her husband and one very naughty dog.

June 2016 | Hardcover | Young Adult | 320 pp | $17.99 | ISBN 9780544805095
HMH Books for Young Readers | hmhco.com | EileenCook.com

CONVERSATION STARTERS

1. Jill is an unreliable narrator. As a reader do you believe her story? Do you think she believes what she says? How does she compare to other unreliable narrators such as Amy in *Gone Girl* and Rachel in *The Girl on the Train*?

2. The story of *With Malice* combines chapters told from Jill's point of view as well as chapters from other characters, news stories and police reports. How did these different viewpoints shape your opinion of what happened in the book?

3. Jill worries that when she goes away to college she will lose her friendship with Simone. Do you have anyone in your life that used to be a very close friend, who you have grown apart from? Would you change that if you could? Do friendships have a time limit?

4. Do you believe that Jill's parents believe she is innocent? Why or why not?

5. Would you consider Jill and Simone to be friends? What role does envy play in friendships? Have you ever had a friendship that wasn't healthy—how did it resolve itself?

6. Once the story of Simone's death hits the press, many people in the public decide that Jill is guilty. Do you think media coverage influences the justice system? How? Do you find you have strong opinions on people in the news?

7. Anna tells Jill that even if she wasn't tough before the experience of being in the rehab hospital will make her tough. How do you think this experience changes Jill?

8. Do you believe Jill's brain injury prevents her from remembering the accident, or is it that she doesn't want to face what really happened?

9. Jill was bothered by an online troll when she wrote her blog. Do you think online bullying is better or worse than being bullied in person? Why? Have you ever had a negative experience online?

10. Because of her brain injury, Jill is vulnerable to having false memories. Do you believe at the end of the book that what she experiences is a dream or a memory? If it is a memory—is Jill justified in deciding to say nothing?

WOLF BY WOLF
Ryan Graudin

Her story begins on a train.

The year is 1956, and the Axis powers of the Third Reich and Imperial Japan rule. To commemorate their Great Victory, they host the Axis Tour: an annual motorcycle race across their conjoined continents. The prize? An audience with the highly reclusive Adolf Hitler at the Victor's Ball in Tokyo.

Yael, a former death camp prisoner, has witnessed too much suffering, and the five wolves tattooed on her arm always remind her of the loved ones she lost. The resistance has given Yael one goal: Win the race and kill Hitler. With the power to skinshift, Yael must complete her mission by impersonating last year's only female racer, Adele Wolfe. But as Yael grows closer to the other competitors, can she be as ruthless as she needs to be to avoid discovery and stay true to her mission?

"Wild and gorgeous, vivid and consuming. I loved it! I can't wait for the sequel."
—**Laini Taylor**, *The New York Times* **bestselling author of the** *Daughter of Smoke & Bone*

BLOOD FOR BLOOD

For the resistance in 1950s Germany, the war may be over, but the fight has just begun. Death camp survivor Yael is on the run. This gripping, thought-provoking sequel to *Wolf by Wolf* will grab readers by the throat with its cinematic writing, fast-paced action, and heart-stopping twists.

ABOUT THE AUTHOR: **Ryan Graudin** was born in Charleston, South Carolina, with a severe case of wanderlust. When she's not traveling, she's busy writing and spending time with her husband and wolf dog. She is the author of the All That Glows series and *Walled City*.

Wolf by Wolf
October 2016 | Paperback | Young Adult | 400 pp | $9.99 | ISBN 9780316405089
Blood for Blood
November 2016 | Hardcover | Young Adult | 496 pp | $17.99 | ISBN 9780316405157
Little, Brown Books for Young Readers | TheNovl.com | RyanGraudin.com

CONVERSATION STARTERS
WOLF BY WOLF

1. Why is it important for Yael to know who she is "on the inside" (46)?

2. What is the meaning of the title? Why does Yael trace the wolves on her arm? Why is it important the wolves are "the only thing about her that stay the same"?

3. How do the ideas of fear and courage connect throughout the book?

4. Why is the structure of the book ("now" vs. "then") important to the story? How did it effect how you read the book?

5. Felix tells Yael as Adele, "Maybe the world is wrong, but you don't have to be the one to save it ... Some things are too broken to be fixed." What do you think of his reflection related to the story and to how you choose to live your life?

BLOOD FOR BLOOD

1. The sequel structure includes a prelude, four parts, and two interludes. What did the prelude and interlude provide? How do they inform the story in the four parts?

2. Luka hears Yael's name for the first time on page 67. Why is the name so unfamiliar and unique to him? Why does he not realize until page 188 when he hears Miriam's name why the names sound so different? Why are names so important throughout the book?

3. On page 193 when Yael asks Luka why he didn't join the resistance, he asks, "Why choose to get crushed when you can survive?" and Yael responds, "Some of us never had that choice." How has fear affected Luka's life and Yael's life differently?

4. On page 332, Luka realizes the enormous differences between his childhood struggles and Yael's. He tells Yael, "It must seem so small to you." And Yael responds, "No person's life is small." Why is this sentence so important to the meaning of the overall book?

5. When Yael visits the artist for her final two tattoos, he tells her not to pay: "What are two more wolves compared to a new start?" How do you think Yael feels about the sacrifices and deaths that were made for this "new start"? He also says, "It will take time to heal just like all the others." What else does this relate to besides the physical tattoos?

WRECKED
Maria Padian

The gut-wrenching, powerful narrative of a college freshman's sexual assault on campus and its aftermath.

Everyone has a different version of what happened that night at MacCallum College. Haley was already in bed when her roommate, Jenny, arrived home shellshocked from the wild Conundrum House party. Richard heard his housemate Jordan brag about the cute freshman he hooked up with. When Jenny accuses Jordan of rape, Haley and Richard find themselves pushed onto opposite sides of the school's investigation. But conflicting interests fueling conflicting versions of the story may make bringing the truth to light nearly impossible.

Maria Padian offers a kaleidoscopic view of a sexual assault on a college campus. *Wrecked* will leave readers thinking about how memory and identity, what's at stake, and who sits in judgment shape what we all decide to believe about the truth.

"Outstanding, powerful, and important ... This is, hands down, one of the best sexual assault reads in YA, and it's a book that high schoolers of all genders should read." —**Kelly Jensen, Book Riot**

"In the face of recent college rape trials, readers will be rapt ... An important, devastating new perspective on an all-too-timely subject." —*Kirkus Reviews*

"Revelatory, deeply real, and urgently important." —**Nova Ren Suma, author of** *The Walls Around Us*

ABOUT THE AUTHOR: **Maria Padian** is a graduate of Middlebury College (BA) and the University of Virginia (MA). She is a freelance writer, essayist, and author of young adult novels, including *Brett McCarthy: Work in Progress*, *Jersey Tomatoes Are the Best*, and *Out of Nowhere*. Maria lives with her family in Brunswick, Maine.

October 2016 | Hardcover | Young Adult | 368 pp | $17.95 | ISBN 9781616206246
Algonquin Young Readers | AlgonquinYoungReaders.com | MariaPadian.com

CONVERSATION STARTERS

1. What does the "fishing" metaphor on pages 41 and 42 tell us about Jordan's attitude toward sex and women? What does the metaphor about college as a "buffet" mean?

2. Once Jenny reports the rape, to what extent is she free to make her own choices about everything that follows? Who respects her boundaries? Who pushes them?

3. On page 146, Richard expresses the idea that sometimes, "yes the night before turns into no the morning after." What is the difference between this perception and what happened to Jenny?

4. On page 48, Jenny wonders, "How come I didn't fight him off?" We later learn why: her body froze in panic. This is a common physiological stress response among sexual assault survivors—not "fight or flight," but "freeze." How does Jenny's behavior during the assault—saying, "I'm so tired," passing out, and being paralyzed—compare with the behavior of a person who is enthusiastically consenting to sex? If a person's consent is not verbal, are there any other ways they might communicate "yes"?

5. On page 170, Haley notes "Jenny was complicated." What does Jenny say or do that leads Haley to that conclusion? How does what happens to Jenny influence how others around her interact with her and/or perceive her?

6. If you were named as a witness by either side in this case and had to speak with the dean, would that be an easy conversation? What might you be worried about? What do you think of Dean Hunt's comment that witnesses seemed more concerned with protecting themselves than with the truth?

7. What do you think of Dean Hunt's efforts to have the accused students withdraw? Would it surprise you to learn that, in reality, only about 10-30% of college students who are found responsible for sexual misconduct, are expelled?

8. What is "wrecked" in the story? What does Richard mean when he says, "I think this was broken beyond repair" (351)?

9. What does Richard think about the idea of asking, "Can I kiss you?" before Matt Trainor's consent presentation? What does he think about it afterward?

BOOK GROUP FAVORITES FROM 2015

In 2016, we asked thousands of book groups to tell us what books they read and discussed during 2015 that they enjoyed most. The top titles were:

FICTION

Orphan Train
Christine Baker Kline |
William Morrow

Me Before You
Jojo Moyes | Penguin Books

The Storied Life of A.J. Fikry
Gabrielle Zevin |
Algonquin Books

The Girl on the Train
Paula Hawkins | Riverhead

The Light Between Oceans
M.L. Stedman | Scribner

The Paris Architect
Charles Belfoure | Sourcebooks

The Invention of Wings
Sue Monk Kidd | Penguin Books

The Goldfinch
Donna Tartt |
Little, Brown & Co

Station Eleven
Emily Mandel | Vintage

The Signature of All Things
Elizabeth Gilbert |
Penguin Books

Americanah
Chimamamanda Ngozi Adichie |
Anchor

Euphoria
Lily King | Grove Press

NONFICTION

Unbroken
Laura Hillenbrand
| Random House

The Boys in the Boat
Daniel James Brown
| Penguin Books

Dead Wake
Erik Larson | Broadway Books

Wild
Cheryl Strayed | Vintage

Being Mortal
Atul Gawande | Henry Holt

H is for Hawk
Helen Macdonald | Grove Press

The Glass Castle
Jeanette Walls | Scribner

Can't We Talk About Something More Pleasant?
Roz Chast | Bloomsbury

It Was Me All Along
Andie Mitchell | Clarkson Potter

Pandora's DNA
Lizzie Stark |
Chicago Review Press

The Underground Girls of Kabul
Jenny Nordberg |
Broadway Books

They Poured Fire On Us From the Sky
Alphonsion Deng, Benson Deng,
Benjamin Ajak | Public Affairs

YOUNG ADULT

The Book Thief
Markus Zusak | Knopf

The Hunger Games
Suzanne Collins | Scholastic

Wonder
R.J. Palacio |
Knopf Books for Young Readers

We Were Liars
Emily Lockhart | Delacorte Press

Miss Peregrine's Home for Peculiar Children
Ransom Riggs | Quirk Books

Hollow City
Ransom Riggs | Quirk Books

The Hired Girl
Laura Amy Schlitz |
Candlewick Press

The Strange and Beautiful Sorrows of Ava Lavender
Leslye Walton | Candlewick Press

The Thing About Jellyfish
Ali Benjamin |
Little, Brown Young Readers

Egg & Spoon
Gregory Maguire |
Candlewick Press

The Silenced
James DeVita |
Milkweed Editions

Please visit ReadingGroupChoices.com between January 1 and April 1, 2017 to enter our 2016 Favorite Books Contest by telling us about your favorite books of 2016. You will be entered for a chance to win bookstore gift certificates to use towards your meetings plus books for each person in your group, compliments of our publishing partners.

READING GROUP
CHOICES

Selections for Lively Discussions

GUIDELINES FOR LIVELY BOOK DISCUSSIONS

1. RESPECT SPACE - Avoid "crosstalk" or talking over others.

2. ALLOW SPACE - Some of us are more outgoing and others more reserved. If you've had a chance to talk, allow others time to offer their thoughts as well.

3. BE OPEN - Keep an open mind, learn from others, and acknowlege there are differences in opinon. That's what makes it interesting!

4. OFFER NEW THOUGHTS - Try not to repeat what others have said, but offer a new perspective.

5. STAY ON THE TOPIC - Contribute to the flow of conversation by holding your comments to the topic of the book, keeping personal references to an appropriate medium.

Great Books ⁓ Great People ⁓ Great Conversation

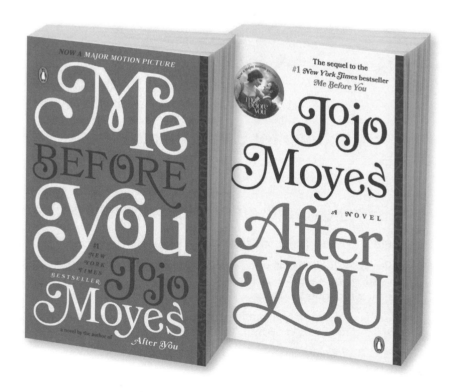 

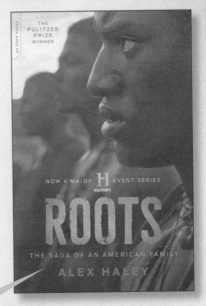

DO YOU LOVE TO READ?

Spread the joy of reading and build a sense of community by starting a Little Free Library book exchange!

Hailed by the *New York Times* as "a global sensation", Little Free Library book exchanges are "take a book, return a book" gathering places where neighbors share their favorite literature and stories.

LITTLE FREE LIBRARY.org ®
TAKE A BOOK · RETURN A BOOK

Find locations near you and learn how to start your own at *www.littlefreelibrary.org*

**READING GROUP
CHOICES**

READING GROUP CHOICES' ADVISORY BOARD

Charlie Mead owned and managed Reading Group Choices from 2005 until 2014. He sold the business to Mary Morgan in April 2014. Charlie's business partner and wife, Barbara Drummond Mead, co-owned and managed the business until her passing in 2011. From 1972 to 1999, Charlie served at Digital Equipment Corporation (DEC) and Compaq Computer Corporation, both now part of Hewlett Packard, most recently as vice president of communication accounts worldwide. In 1999, Charlie became vice president of Sales of Interpath Communications Corporation, an Internet infrastructure company, until the company's sale in 2000. From 2000 to 2005, Charlie owned and managed Connxsys LLC, a communications consulting firm.

Donna Paz Kaufman founded Reading Group Choices in 1994 to connect publishers, booksellers, libraries, and readers with great books for group discussion. Today, the bookstore training and consulting group of Paz & Associates is fully dedicated to assisting people around the globe open, manage, and sell their independent bookstores. To learn more about Paz & Associates, visit PazBookBiz.com.

Mark Nichols was an independent bookseller in various locations from Maine to Connecticut from 1976 through 1993. After seven years in a variety of positions with major publishers in New York and San Francisco, he joined the American Booksellers Association in 2000, and currently serves as Development Officer. He is on the Board of James Patterson's ReadKiddoRead.com, and has edited two volumes with Newmarket Press: *Book Sense Best Books* (2004) and *Book Sense Best Children's Books* (2005).

John Mutter is editor-in-chief of *Shelf Awareness*, the daily e-mail newsletter focusing on books, media about books, retailing and related issues to help booksellers, librarians and others do their jobs more effectively. Before he and his business partner, Jenn Risko, founded the company in May 2005, he was executive editor of bookselling at *Publishers Weekly*. He has covered book industry issues for 25 years and written for a variety of publications, including *The Bookseller* in the U.K.; *Australian Bookseller & Publisher*; *Boersenblatt*, the German book trade magazine;

and *College Store Magazine* in the U.S. For more information about *Shelf Awareness*, go to its website, shelf-awareness.com.

Megan Hanson's background includes extensive customer service work, experience coordinating marketing campaigns for the Madrid-based NGO Colegas, plus serving as a Community Literacy Coordinator for the Madison non-profit Literacy Network. Since 2012, she has been working for the internationally-recognized non-profit Little Free Library, helping them to develop and scale to meet demand. Her focus is on digital marketing, data and web management, product development and customer service.

René Martin is the Events Director/Publicist at Quail Ridge Books in Raleigh, NC. "Nancy Olson, who owned and operated Quail Ridge Books & Music from 1981 until it was sold in 2013, hired me in 2000. I knew nothing about the book business, but said yes, it would be fun. And it has been! Sixteen years later I now know a little more about the book business, and love being the events coordinator/publicist for Quail Ridge Books. We now host almost 300 events a year. My goal is to make QRB a model publicity department, and we'll have a beautiful, new store in which to make that happen."

Nicole Sullivan opened BookBar, a community bookstore wine bar in 2013. Immediately recognizing a need to connect readers with book clubs in their area, she then founded bookclubhub.org in 2014. BookBed, an author bed & breakfast located just above the book store opened its doors in Fall of 2015. Additionally, she has funneled her passion for helping others to create successful bookstore / bar & cafe models through her work as a consultant with Paz & Associates. Nicole proudly serves as co-President and founder of her neighborhood business association, Tennyson Berkeley Business Association (TBBA) and as Treasurer of her local maintenance district for the city of Denver.

ORDER YOUR COPIES OF READING GROUP CHOICES!

HOW MANY COPIES OF EACH EDITION WOULD YOU LIKE TO RECEIVE?

___ 2017 ___ 2016 ___ 2015 ___ 2014 ___ 2013 ___ 2012 ___ 2011 ___ 2010 ___ 2008 ___ 2006 ___ 2005 ___ 2004

PRICING:

☐ 1-4 copies = $7.95/copy
☐ 5-24 copies = $4.75/copy
☐ 25 or more = $3.95/copy

SHIPPING & HANDLING:

☐ $2.50 for up to 5 copies
☐ $5.00 for 6-10 copies
☐ $7.50 for 11-20 copies
☐ $10.00 for over 20 copies

WI RESIDENTS:

☐ 5.5% sales tax

TOTAL COST OF COPIES: _____ + COST OF SHIPPING: _____ + TAX IF APPLICABLE: _____ = TOTAL: _____

PAYMENT:

☐ Check enclosed   ☐ Credit Card (VISA, MC, Discover)

Card Number _____ Exp Date _____

Signature _____

SHIPPING ADDRESS:

_____

_____

_____ City _____ State _____ Zip _____

PLEASE MAIL FORM TO: Reading Group Choices • 113 Bascom Pl • Madison, WI 53726
FOR MORE INFO: info@ReadingGroupChoices.com